Educational Leadership for Transformation and Social Justice

Educational Leadership for Transformation and Social Justice examines the relationship between the lived experiences of educational leaders at the University of the Free State in South Africa and how they think about and practice leadership for transformation and social justice. Based on biographical information, public speeches, published writings, and in-depth, semi-structured, face-to-face interviews, the book presents and analyzes seven chapter-length narratives of these leaders.

This book explores how some leaders at the University of the Free State – from the vantage point of various racialized and gendered identities, and generational experiences – conceptualize and enact leadership for transformation and social justice. Ambrosio argues that there are certain values, beliefs, concepts, principles, and ways of thinking that cut across their experiences and demographic differences. The narratives are presented in the leaders' own words, describe how their lived experiences shaped their values and identities, and inform how they think about and practice leadership for transformation and social justice. One convergence that emerged among these leaders is that their leadership is an extension of who they are – of their core values, identities and ethical commitments. Another is that they are motivated by visions of change that go beyond the university, by bigger dreams that infuse their work with meaning and purpose.

With its in-depth analysis of the narratives, this book will provide educational leaders who have an orientation toward transformation and social justice with insights that enable them to think differently about how to make the policies, programs, and institutional culture of their own universities more equitable and just. It will appeal to academics, researchers, and postgraduate students in the fields of education, educational justice, higher education, educational leadership and change, social justice, and racial justice.

John Ambrosio is associate professor of social foundations in the Department of Educational Studies at Ball State University. He received a Core Fulbright Scholar Program grant to work with colleagues in the Faculty of Education at the University of the Free State in South Africa. Dr. Ambrosio's most recent publication, coauthored with Adré le Roux and Percy Mdunge, is "Re-visioning Teacher Education for Social Justice in Post-Apartheid South Africa" in Social Justice and Transformative Learning: Culture and Identity in the United States and South Africa, edited by Saundra M. Tomlinson-Clarke and Darren L. Clarke.

Routledge Research in Educational Leadership series

Books in this series

Political Philosophy, Educational Administration and Educative Leadership
Reynold Macpherson

Educational Administration and Leadership
Theoretical Foundations
Edited by David Burgess and Paul Newton

Indigenous Leadership in Higher Education
Edited by Robin Starr Minthorn and Alicia Fedelina Chávez

Student Voice and School Governance
Distributing Leadership to Youth and Adults
Mark Brasof

Leading for Change
Race, intimacy and leadership on divided university campuses
Jonathan Jansen

Restoring Justice in Urban Schools
Disrupting the School-to-Prison Pipeline
Anita Wadhwa

Generational Identity, Educational Change, and School Leadership
Corrie Stone-Johnson

Educational Leadership in Becoming
Nuraan Davids and Yusef Waghid

Educational Leadership for Transformation and Social Justice
Narratives of change in South Africa
John Ambrosio

Educational Leadership for Transformation and Social Justice
Narratives of change in South Africa

John Ambrosio

LONDON AND NEW YORK

First published 2017
by Routledge
2 Park Square, Milton Park, Abingdon, Oxon OX14 4RN

and by Routledge
711 Third Avenue, New York, NY 10017

First issued in paperback 2018

Routledge is an imprint of the Taylor & Francis Group, an informa business

© 2017 John Ambrosio

The right of John Ambrosio to be identified as author of this work
has been asserted by him in accordance with sections 77 and 78 of the
Copyright, Designs and Patents Act 1988.

All rights reserved. No part of this book may be reprinted or
reproduced or utilised in any form or by any electronic, mechanical,
or other means, now known or hereafter invented, including
photocopying and recording, or in any information storage or
retrieval system, without permission in writing from the publishers.

Trademark notice: Product or corporate names may be trademarks
or registered trademarks, and are used only for identification and
explanation without intent to infringe.

British Library Cataloguing in Publication Data
A catalogue record for this book is available from the British Library

Library of Congress Cataloging in Publication Data
Names: Ambrosio, John, 1957– author.
Title: Educational leadership for transformation and social justice :
    narratives of change in South Africa / John Ambrosio.
Description: Abingdon, Oxon ; New York, NY : Routledge, 2017.
Identifiers: LCCN 2016025357 | ISBN 9781138923539 (hardcover) |
    ISBN 9781315685045 (electronic)
Subjects: LCSH: University of the Free State—Administration. |
    Educational leadership—South Africa. | Educational change—South
    Africa. | Social justice—Study and teaching (Higher)—South Africa. |
    College administrators—South Africa—Biography.
Classification: LCC LG451.B5 A64 2017 | DDC 371.20968—dc23
LC record available at https://lccn.loc.gov/2016025357

ISBN 13: 978-1-138-60220-5 (pbk)
ISBN 13: 978-1-138-92353-9 (hbk)

Typeset in Galliard
by Apex CoVantage, LLC

To my parents, Saverio and Angela Ambrosio, whose sacrifices and hopes made whatever I have achieved in life possible; to my wife, Jacqueline, for her unflagging support and encouragement throughout this project; and for Isaac, for being a young man we are proud to call our son

Contents

Acknowledgements	ix
Introduction	1
1 What is educational leadership for transformation and social justice? JOHN AMBROSIO	3
2 The soft revolution: Embracing the better versions of ourselves JONATHAN JANSEN	10
3 The question of fairness: Creating opportunities to succeed M.G. SECHABA MAHLOMAHOLO	30
4 Something much bigger: Doing what is good and what is right B.R. RUDI BUYS	53
5 Repairing the brokenness of the past: Working through the unfinished business of trauma PUMLA GOBODO-MADIKIZELA	76
6 There is nobody innocent here: Shared complicity and the sharp edge of social justice ANDRÉ KEET	94
7 Transformation as an intellectual and ethical project: Changing inherited patterns of thought and social practice LIS LANGE	112

viii *Contents*

8 **A new hope: Believing in a fairer, more decent, and more humane society** 127

JOHN SAMUEL

9 **A bigger dream: Visions of educational leadership for transformation and social justice in South Africa** 143

JOHN AMBROSIO

Acknowledgements

I want to thank Professor Dennis Francis, former dean of the Faculty of Education, for hosting me as a Fulbright Scholar, and my colleagues in the Faculty of Education, especially Dr. Molebatsi Nkoane, and others at the University of the Free State, for so graciously welcoming a stranger into their community and making him feel at home. I also want to express my immense gratitude to the educational leaders who participated in this study, and to the J. William Fulbright Foreign Scholarship Board for providing me with a Core Fulbright Scholar Program award, which made this book possible.

Introduction

There is a burgeoning crisis in public schools and institutions of higher education in South Africa. As Jonathan Jansen, the internationally renowned vice chancellor and rector of the University of the Free State warned in a public lecture: "If we do not stop the free fall in education within the next 10 to 15 years, this democracy will implode and all chances of creating an economically productive and humanely compassionate society will be lost" (Jansen, 2012, p. 10). Creating opportunities for previously marginalized and excluded people to access institutions of higher education, and to be academically successful, is crucial to the social and economic development of South Africa and to strengthening its nascent democratic culture.

After months of demonstrations, in October and November 2015 the crisis in higher education reached a boiling point, and student protests erupted at universities across South Africa. Students demanded a reduction or elimination of university fees and called on various universities to eliminate structural inequalities, remove colonial symbols, end the outsourcing of university services, and discontinue the use of Afrikaans as a language of instruction.

The persistence of extreme poverty and inequality in South Africa has created a situation in which the majority of students on university campuses, approximately 80% of whom are black, are unable to afford university fees or accommodations given the severe shortage of residential housing at most universities. Students from poor families may receive bursaries (scholarships) to attend a university, but they typically do not cover all of their expenses, while students from many middle-class families cannot afford university fees but do not qualify for assistance from the National Student Financial Aid Scheme, which has insufficient resources to fund all of the students who qualify. Despite the lack of adequate funding, students are required to pay fees before they can register for classes at most institutions and must repay outstanding debts before they can graduate. As a result, financial constraints contribute significantly to the exceedingly high dropout rate, especially for black students. In 2014, the average graduation rate for undergraduate students in South Africa's 25 public institutions of higher education was only 16% (Department of Higher Education and Training, 2016, p. 17).

This book aims to contribute to the cultivation of educational leaders who are committed to transformation and social justice in institutions of higher education

2 Introduction

in South Africa and other post-conflict societies. To this end, I interviewed seven leaders at the University of the Free State to examine the relationship between their lived experience and how they conceptualize and practice leadership for transformation and social justice and to identify some commonalities: key ideas, concepts, values, and beliefs that inform their leadership.

Of course, educational leaders must work within a larger social, economic, and political context that frames and constrains the parameters of possibility. Nonetheless, they can influence the culture and climate of their institutions and make strategic policy decisions that move them toward greater access and equity.

In Chapter One I examine notions of transformation and social justice that drive progressive change at the University of the Free State and delineate the context of educational leadership. Chapters Two through Eight contain separate profiles of the seven leaders, which include: Jonathan Jansen, the vice chancellor and rector; M.G. Sechaba Mahlomaholo, dean of the Faculty of Education; B.R. Rudi Buys, former dean of Student Affairs; Pumla Gobodo-Madikizela, former director of the interdisciplinary program in Trauma, Forgiveness, and Reconciliation; André Keet, director of the Institute for Reconciliation and Social Justice; Lis Lange, acting vice rector (academic) and director of the Directorate for Institutional Research and Academic Planning; and John Samuel, former interim director of the Institute for Reconciliation and Social Justice and senior advisor to Jonathan Jansen. In Chapter Nine I examine ways of thinking about leadership that cut across the different narratives.

The chapter-long profiles consist mostly of conversations between myself and the individual leaders. My hope is that these personal stories, told by the leaders themselves, which examine their moral, intellectual, and political development, how they conceptualize and practice leadership, and how their lived experience informs their ethical choices and moral actions will be of interest to readers. Ultimately, my aim is to enable leaders in institutions of higher education in South Africa and other post-conflict societies grappling with historical memory and trauma, and a legacy of racial oppression, to think differently about their practice.

Despite the enormous challenges of leading for transformation and social justice in this context, the leaders profiled in this book continue to work toward realizing the values and ideals enshrined in the South African Constitution and fulfilling its promise of a more just, decent, and humane country.

References

Department of Higher Education and Training. (2016). *Statistics on post-school education and training in South Africa: 2014*. Retrieved from http://www.dhet.gov.za/ DHET%20Statistics%20Publication/Statistics%20on%20Post-School%20Educa tion%20and%20Training%20in%20South%20Africa%202014.pdf

Jansen, J. (2012). *The mathematics of democracy: The 2012 Helen Suzman memorial lecture*. Retrieved from http://www.ufs.ac.za/docs/default-source/all-documents/ prof-jonathan-jansen_2012-helen-suzman-memorial-lecture-1079-eng.pdf?sfvrsn=0

1 What is educational leadership for transformation and social justice?

John Ambrosio

Educational leadership for transformation and social justice must be rooted in the particular social and historical conditions in which it is practiced. As such, there is no single unifying, one-size-fits-all or all-encompassing notion of what it means. While there are certain values, ethical principles, and beliefs that may inform their work, educational leaders who seek transformation and social justice must respond to the inherent contradictions and problems that emerge within a particular social formation at a certain moment in time. That is, the meanings of transformation and social justice are constituted and delimited by the specific conditions and circumstances that define the context of leadership, which are always changing.

While the concepts of transformation and social justice are not synonymous, they intersect in important ways. In contemporary South Africa, especially in institutions of higher education, transformation is a highly politicized and contested concept. For Jonathan Jansen, the internationally renowned vice chancellor and rector of the University of the Free State (UFS), transformation refers to changes in social relations and how individuals and social groups view and interact with one another, especially with regard to race, and to changing the institutional culture of the university to make it more welcoming and inclusive. On the other hand, social justice is concerned with redressing past injustices, that is, righting the wrongs of centuries of exploitation and oppression by ensuring a just and equitable distribution of resources and opportunities for previously excluded and marginalized individuals and social groups.

Professor Jansen, as students and staff typically call him, frames his leadership goals in terms of two major initiatives: the Human and Academic Projects. The Human Project seeks to transform the nature and quality of human relations on the campus, especially among people who have been racialized differently, to create a more humane and inclusive climate, whereas the Academic Project focuses on the drive for academic excellence, which includes raising academic standards, attracting high-performing students, providing students and faculty with opportunities for personal growth and professional development, and cultivating a rigorous and vibrant intellectual culture at the UFS. In this way, his vision of change is similar to the notion of transformative leadership articulated by Shields (2011), which "emphasizes the need for education to focus both on academic excellence and social transformation" (p. 4).

4 John Ambrosio

However, transforming the social relations and institutional culture of the UFS will not be successful unless issues of social justice are seriously addressed. In postapartheid South Africa educational leaders must focus not only on transforming human relations, on changing the way people see and treat one another, but on transforming relations of power and privilege. These two goals are ineluctable: changing the hearts, minds, and cultural practices of people in a post-conflict society like South Africa, with a long history of racial oppression and exclusion, cannot succeed in the absence of a demonstrable and sustained commitment to social justice. Thus, leaders of institutions of higher education in South Africa must pursue transformation and social justice simultaneously and walk a fine line in seeking both reconciliation *and* redress.

A key aim of this book is to illuminate the relation between the lived and embodied experience of some leaders at the UFS and how they understand and enact leadership for transformation and social justice. To this end, I prepared chapter-long narratives of seven educational leaders based on biographical information and in-depth, semi-structured, face-to-face interviews I conducted as a Fulbright Scholar in the Faculty of Education from March to June 2014. I was drawn to the UFS by the international reputation of its vice chancellor and rector, Jonathan Jansen, and the leading role it plays among universities in South Africa in institutional transformation and integration. The UFS is the first historically Afrikaans university to fully embrace a nonracial vision of South Africa and is pioneering efforts to improve access and equity for previously excluded and marginalized people.

The educational leaders included in this book are situated in various places in the organizational structure and hierarchy of the UFS. Because they have different racialized and gendered identities, as well as generational experiences, their perspectives reflect the lived experience of leaders from a range of social and historical locations. Despite this, as I argue in Chapter Nine, there are certain concepts, values, principles, and ways of thinking that inform their approaches to leadership. Thus, in addition to examining the relation between their lived experience and leadership practices, a central aim of this book is to identify ways of conceptualizing and practicing leadership for transformation and social justice that can inform and contribute to the work of leaders in institutions of higher education in South Africa and elsewhere. My hope is that these narratives will encourage and inspire other leaders to critically reflect on their practice and to incorporate, in whatever way makes sense in their particular contexts, the lessons and insights they derive from these narratives.

Regardless of the context, leadership for transformation and social justice requires moral courage and a willingness to challenge what is for what should be. It often means going against the grain, advocating for unpopular causes, and taking both personal and professional risks. As I discovered, their embrace of leadership for transformation and social justice is less a conscious choice than a natural expression of their core values, identities, and lived experiences.

While scholarship on leadership for social justice has increased significantly in the United States and elsewhere over the past 15 years, there remains a dearth of research on leadership regarding institutions of higher education in South

Africa. This project was inspired, in part, by the work of Professor Jansen, who has written extensively on the emotional, psychological, and political costs and challenges of "leading against the grain" in postapartheid South Africa (Jansen, 2005, 2009). In his work, Professor Jansen emphasizes the importance of employing a biographical lens and examining the underlying values and beliefs that inform how educational leaders think in seeking to understand what motivates their leadership (Jansen, 2006).

Rather than tell other people's stories, it is important that these leaders speak for themselves in their own words. Thus, after providing some biographical information and relevant context, the narratives consist mostly of conversations between myself and the individual leaders. While I explored some of the same issues with each of the leaders, I also posed questions that were specific to their lived experiences, public lectures, and various publications. All of the interviews were conducted in English. Although English is the official lingua franca of public life at the UFS, it is not the mother tongue of most of these leaders.

It is important to note that I did not approach this research as a neutral or disinterested observer but as someone with a long-standing and deep commitment to promoting equity and social justice in schools and society. As a white male university professor from the United States, who benefits from white racial privilege and male privilege in both the United States and South Africa, I was acutely aware of my social location within South African society. My privileged position as a white male from North America was always foregrounded in my consciousness when interacting with South African colleagues. During the year I spent at the UFS (August 2013–July 2014), I developed personal and professional relationships with some of the leaders in this book and had many opportunities to participate in university events, including the summer and autumn graduation ceremonies, the Open Day welcoming assembly, as well as numerous public lectures, conferences, colloquia, discussions, and informal social gatherings.

The transformation process at the UFS is supported by an infrastructure of institutes, research centers, and degree programs that include the Institute for Reconciliation and Social Justice; the cross-disciplinary program on Trauma, Forgiveness, and Reconciliation; the Center for Research on Higher Education and Development; and the Institute for Institutional Research and Academic Planning. The transformation process is also advanced through various university initiatives such as the F1 Leadership for Change study abroad program, which sends a group of first-year students to universities in the United States, Europe, and Asia for two weeks every year to learn about other cultures, and the Prestige Scholars' program, which provides some newer scholars with research assistance, financial support, and faculty mentors. Together, these programs and others aim to transform the institutional culture of the UFS by changing the dominant norms, values, and practices and by producing a cadre of student leaders and a new generation of scholars with an orientation toward social justice.

One of the hallmarks of Professor Jansen's leadership is that the recruitment of high-performing students, the distribution of bursaries (scholarships), and inclusion in initiatives like the F1 Leadership for Change program are allocated on

6   *John Ambrosio*

a nonracial basis. He is deeply committed to supporting all students in need, whatever their racial assignment, and to maintaining a diverse student body at the UFS. To this end, Professor Jansen donated part of his first year's salary, and the profits from two of his best-selling books, to provide bursaries for students.

I chose to privilege the voices of these educational leaders in the narratives because it can potentially reveal, better than stories *about* them, the meaning and essence of their thoughts. In my reading of various collections of interviews with leading figures in literature and philosophy, I found that something significant is often illuminated in the ebb and flow of dialogue, in the ordinary back and forth of conversation, that may not otherwise be accessible (Lotringer, 1996; Taylor-Guthrie, 1994). The sheer randomness and unpredictability of dialogue can open a window into a person's reasoning process and motivations.

The socioeconomic context

While a political revolution took place in 1994 in South Africa that led to the establishment of the first democratically elected government, many analysts argue that the political revolution was not accompanied by a similar transformation of the economic system (Alexander, 2013; Bundy, 2014; Terreblanche, 2012). While a relatively small black elite and middle class emerged after the transition to democracy, most of the wealth, income, and economic power remains in the hands of the Afrikaner minority. In its final report, the Truth and Reconciliation Commission recommended a one-time wealth tax on corporate and private income to address extreme inequality in South African society, but it was ignored. As a result, the majority of blacks, who constitute more than 80% of the population, continue to live in conditions of abject poverty.

One of the challenges for the African National Congress, the dominant political party in South Africa since the end of apartheid, has been to create enough jobs that pay a living wage to satisfy the fast-growing and relatively young population and to adequately prepare working-age people to participate in the labor market. In 2013, South Africa had an official unemployment rate of more than 25%, which does not account for workers who are available but have given up looking for work. When these workers are included in an expanded definition of unemployment, the rate is nearly 37% (Statistics South Africa, 2016). Thus, South Africa has an unemployment rate that far exceeds the worst years of the Great Depression in the United States, which is the new normal. This extraordinarily high unemployment rate also has a racial dimension: unemployment is four times higher for blacks than whites.

In 2013, about one-third of 15- to 24-year-olds in South Africa, about 3.5 million youth were neither employed nor in school or training (Statistics South Africa, 2016). Many of these young people dropped out of severely under-resourced and largely dysfunctional public schools before taking matric (the high school graduation exam) in 11th grade and thus have few economic opportunities. Nearly one-third of South Africans, and about 46% of all households, receive at least one social security grant from the national government, which are small monthly payments for old age, child support, foster care, dependency care, and disabilities (South African Info, 2014). Often, entire households survive on the social grant of one family member.

The educational context

Despite spending nearly 6% of its gross domestic product (GDP) on public education, which is relatively high when compared to other nations of similar size (but less so given that 15–24-year-olds comprise more than 20% of the population), many public schools that serve the poorest students, who are predominantly black, remain severely under-resourced and lack basic facilities such as electricity, running water and indoor toilets; school supplies like books and desks; and libraries and science labs (Equal Education, November 14, 2012). In addition, many teachers in these schools are poorly trained, have insufficient content knowledge, and lack a sense of professionalism. As a result, about 80% of all public schools in South Africa, typically in rural areas and townships, are mostly dysfunctional. The combined effect of the deplorable conditions in many public schools is that official claims to the contrary, only about 40% of learners in 2013 passed matric despite the low bar set for passing. Of those who passed, only 16% qualified for university admission (Spaull, 2014).

This context presents enormous challenges for leaders in institutions of higher education in South Africa who seek transformation and social justice. Students who manage to qualify for university admission typically arrive underprepared for college-level work and are in need of significant financial and academic support. To compound the problem, as a dual-medium university, the UFS offers all courses in Afrikaans and English, which means that students who do not speak Afrikaans, who are mostly black, must take classes in English, which is typically not their mother tongue. In South Africa, questions of language and culture have become a proxy for issues of race, power, and privilege, which is why maintaining the Afrikaans language and culture at the UFS has become a primary concern and rallying point for the Afrikaner community and media.

Efforts to change the racial and gender composition of leadership at the university, to make the institutional culture more diverse and inclusive, have run up against persistent opposition from members of the Afrikaner community, who typically see themselves as victims of the new social order, as a persecuted minority whose language and culture are under the threat of extinction. In this emotionally charged context, incidents between whites and blacks are instantly transformed into racial conflicts that provoke outrage and ignite strong passions on all sides.

Thus, educational leaders at institutions of higher education in South Africa have an arduous and potentially explosive road to travel: they must find a way to pursue reconciliation and social justice simultaneously. Whereas reconciliation requires understanding and forgiveness, social justice requires a reallocation of resources, power, and privilege. Educational leaders must continually negotiate the competing and often conflicting demands of the Afrikaner community,

8 *John Ambrosio*

which claims victimization in the postapartheid era, and the black community, which demands immediate access and inclusion, and an equitable distribution of resources and opportunities. Walking this fine line is a daunting task, a balancing act that pleases very few people.

Jonathan Jansen was appointed vice chancellor and rector of the UFS in October 2009 in the midst of what became known as the Reitz incident, in which four white students humiliated five black employees of the university. The incident was videotaped by the students, posted on YouTube, and became the focus of a fierce and bitter national debate about race. Professor Jansen was under tremendous pressure from powerful leaders in the ANC (African National Congress) and elsewhere, who demanded the immediate expulsion and prosecution of the students. In addition, many blacks called for severe penalties for acts of perceived white racism and a faster transition to positions of power for members of previously marginalized and excluded social groups.

Given this situation, educational leaders at institutions of higher education in South Africa are caught between a rock and a hard place: They are harshly criticized by many in the black community if they are viewed as being too lenient in punishing instances of perceived white racism or too slow in transforming the social relations of power and privilege, and they are loudly denounced by many in the Afrikaner community and media if they are viewed as moving too quickly or too far in changing the racial demographics of leadership and the institutional culture of the UFS. The situation in South Africa is reminiscent of the Civil Rights Movement in the United States during the 50s and 60s, when African American leaders faced a similar dilemma.

Educational leaders in South Africa must address the legitimate demands of those who were exploited and oppressed under apartheid and the fears and economic insecurities of the white beneficiaries of apartheid. Walking this fine line is especially challenging given the conflicting narratives of blacks and whites about what actually happened during the apartheid era and the failure of many whites to acknowledge, much less apologize or make restitution for, the oppression of blacks. In addition, the intergenerational transmission of historical memory and trauma in a post-conflict society like South Africa, what Professor Jansen calls 'knowledge in the blood' with regard to Afrikaner students, presents a significant obstacle to achieving reconciliation (Jansen, 2009).

Thus, it is essential that educational leaders in South Africa have the moral integrity and courage to take unpopular positions, to lead against the grain. As Professor Jansen suggests, this requires that leaders know who they are, what their core values and nonnegotiable principles are, and be willing to act in accordance with them, regardless of the consequences. This is the great moral challenge of leadership in higher education in contemporary South Africa.

The international implications of this research are most significant for countries that have a long history of racial oppression and exclusion, especially post-conflict societies seeking a path toward reconciliation and social justice. Although there are important social and historical differences, some striking parallels exist between the racial history of South Africa and the United States and the impact of slavery, colonialism, and segregation on present day inequities in public education.

Both countries continue to grapple with a legacy of racial segregation, exploitation, and oppression in the form of severely under-resourced public schools in poor communities and communities of color, low achievement and educational attainment, a lack of access to higher education, and school and university cultures that do not adequately support and foster the academic success of previously marginalized and excluded students. Since these issues are not unique to the United States or South Africa, this study could have implications for educational leaders in other post-conflict societies that suffer from a history of extreme racialized inequality.

References

Alexander, N. (2013). *Thoughts on the new South Africa*. Auckland Park: Jacana Media.

Bundy, C. (2014). *Short-changed? South Africa since apartheid*. Auckland Park: Jacana Media.

Equal Education. (November 14, 2012). Education video makes waves for taking on Angie. *Mail & Guardian*. Retrieved from http://mg.co.za/article/2012–11–14-education-video-taking-on-angie-makes-waves

Jansen, J. (2005). Black dean: Race, reconciliation and the emotions of deanship. *Harvard Educational Review*, 75(3), 306–326.

Jansen, J. (2006). Leading against the grain: The politics and emotions of leading for social justice in South Africa. *Leadership and Policy in Schools*, 5(1), 37–51.

Jansen, J. (2009). *Knowledge in the blood*. Stanford: Stanford University Press.

Lotringer, S. (Ed.). (1996). *Foucault live: Collected interviews, 1961–1984*. New York: Semiotext(e).

Shields, C. (2011). Transformative leadership: An introduction. In C. Shields (Ed.), *Transformative leadership: A reader* (pp. 1–17). New York: Peter Lang.

South African Info. (2014). Retrieved from http://www.southafrica.info/about/social/grants-190614.htm#.Vu7eoRIrK_t

Spaull, N. (January 10, 2014). Matric is failing SA's lost children. *Mail & Guardian*. Retrieved from http://mg.co.za/article/2014–01–09-matric-is-failing-sas-lost-children

Statistics South Africa. (2016). Retrieved from http://www.statssa.gov.za/?p=1034

Taylor-Guthrie, D. (Ed.). (1994). *Conversations with Toni Morrison*. Jackson: University Press of Mississippi.

Terreblanche, S. (2012). *Lost in transformation: South Africa's search for a new future since 1986*. Standon: KMM Review Publishing Co.

2 The soft revolution
Embracing the better versions of ourselves

Jonathan Jansen

Jonathan Jansen was the vice-chancellor and rector of the University of the Free State (UFS) from October 2009 to August 2016. He is a household name in South Africa and an internationally renowned scholar and educational leader. Professor Jansen was the first black dean at the University of Pretoria, wrote a book about his experience called *Knowledge in the Blood* (2009), and writes a column for *The Times*, a leading national English-language newspaper in South Africa. Some of his columns were collected into two best-selling books, *We Need to Talk* (2011) and *We Need to Act* (2013), in which Professor Jansen sought to ignite and influence public discussion of issues such as education, leadership, and race relations and to inspire hope and citizen action.

Professor Jansen was born in rural Montagu, but grew up in the townships of Retreat and Steenberg in the Cape Flats areas of Cape Town, and was strongly influenced in his early years by the Black Consciousness Movement. From 1979 to 1984 he attended the University of the Western Cape and the University of South Africa, where he earned a teaching diploma and undergraduate degrees in botany and zoology, comparative education, and science education. Professor Jansen went on to earn a master's degree in curriculum and instruction in science education from Cornell University in 1987 and a PhD from the Stanford University School of Education, with a minor in political science, in 1991. He was a Fulbright scholar at Stanford University in 2007 and has received numerous honors, awards, and honorary degrees.

Professor Jansen taught high school biology at Weston High School in the rural Western Cape coastal town of Vredenburg and at Trafalgar High School in Cape Town. He has held various positions: at nongovernmental organizations (NGOs) in South Africa; as a visiting scholar in political science and African studies at Stanford University; as professor and chair of Curriculum Studies and dean of the Faculty of Education at the University of Durban-Westville; and as dean of the Faculty of Education at the University of Pretoria.

Professor Jansen arrived at the UFS in the midst of what became known as the Reitz incident, after the residence hall where it occurred, in which four white students humiliated five black employees of the university. The incident was videotaped by the students, posted on YouTube, and became the focus of a fierce

The soft revolution 11

and divisive national debate about racism. The video appears to show a series of games being played by the students and workers, one of which required the workers to kneel while eating food a student had ostensibly urinated on. As Professor Jansen noted in a *Times* column, the games were actually "a racist attack on the black staff as a means of protesting racial integration in the campus residences" (Jansen, 2013, p. 100).

Professor Jansen was under tremendous pressure from political leaders in the ANC and elsewhere, who demanded the immediate expulsion and prosecution of the students. Since the new democratic dispensation in 1994, many blacks (a term of racial solidarity under apartheid that signifies Africans, coloreds, and Indians) have called for harsher penalties regarding acts of perceived white racism and a faster transition to positions of power and leadership for members of previously marginalized and excluded social groups. Educational leaders are harshly criticized by many in the black community if they are viewed as being too lenient or too slow in transforming the social relations of power and privilege, and they are loudly denounced by the Afrikaner community and media if they are viewed as moving too quickly, or too far, in transforming the racial demographics of leadership and the institutional culture of historically Afrikaner universities like the UFS. Professor Jansen resisted these pressures and, in his inaugural address as the vice chancellor and rector, announced that he was dropping disciplinary charges against the four white students in a gesture of reconciliation and to acknowledge the university's responsibility to create an institutional culture and campus climate in which racism is not tolerated.

In February 2011 the four former students (they had since graduated) and five workers met for the first time since 2008 in the rector's seminar room. After engaging in prolonged and difficult negotiations that sought to avoid "legal remedies for complex human problems," the parties came to an agreement. After offering private apologies, the students read a public apology to the workers in a context of limited media exposure "given the intense emotions, fragility, and vulnerability of the former students and workers" (Jansen, 2013, p. 102). A representative of the university also read an apology to the workers and students, and to all South Africans for mistakes it made in handling the incident.

In 2008 university leaders closed the Reitz residence hall and sought to create a space on the campus to conduct research and engage in critical conversations about racial reconciliation and social justice, which ultimately became known as the Institute for Reconciliation and Social Justice. The Reitz settlement also resulted in the establishment of a Human Rights Desk at the institute, which promotes a culture of human rights on the UFS campus and acts as an ombudsman in resolving possible human rights violations.

Not everyone was happy with Professor Jansen's approach to resolving the situation nor with the outcome. In fact, his position was enormously unpopular, and he was severely criticized by individuals and organizations on both sides of the issue. However, rather than remain mired in racial conflicts, Professor Jansen focused his attention on advancing what he calls the Human and Academic Projects, that is, with cultivating relationships of mutual respect, especially between

12 Johnathan Jansen

black and white students, and pursuing academic excellence by raising admissions standards, recruiting high-performing students, and providing students and faculty with opportunities for personal growth and professional development.

Changing the institutional culture of a university, in a country that remains extremely unequal, divided, and traumatized, often means that educational leaders have to go out on a limb and potentially face harsh criticism. Professor Jansen has argued that the enduring memories and traumas of apartheid, even among the 'born frees' (black students born after the end of apartheid in 1994) means that racial incidents on the campus are likely continue for some time. While addressing them is important, Professor Jansen sought to fundamentally change the social relations and institutional culture of the university.

Professor Jansen's office was on the ground floor of the main administration building on the campus. This was a deliberate choice meant to send a message, especially to students, that the vice chancellor is accessible and does not live in an ivory tower far removed from them. Thus, it was not unusual to see Professor Jansen tending a grill or otherwise serving students, faculty, and staff at various campus events. For him, this is a conscious and deliberate effort to project, both literally and symbolically, a message of humility and accessibility.

One striking aspect of Professor Jansen's leadership is that he has repeatedly apologized in public for perhaps unintentionally hurting or slighting people and has acknowledged not only that all leaders make mistakes but that recognizing and accepting this human reality is central to good leadership. He argues that accepting one's limitations as a broken human being is an essential attribute of leadership, especially in post-conflict societies and that "good leaders are aware of their weaknesses and readily admit to their own sense of struggle with history, memory, and identity" (Jansen, 2011, p. 168). For him, good leadership requires that we know who we are, what our core values are, and have the moral courage to act on them, whatever the consequences. Professor Jansen has repeatedly demonstrated a willingness to take unpopular positions when the deeply held values and beliefs that undergird his leadership are at stake.

Professor Jansen (hereafter JJ) began our conversation by discussing the important distinction between social justice and transformation in his notion of leadership.

JJ: I've just written a piece which is an attempt to untangle concepts of social justice from concepts of transformation because I think very often South Africans use both to mean the same or similar things. The process causes all kinds of chaos. For me, social justice in the context of a country like South Africa is an attempt to correct something that was wrong. For example, when I hire a black, or attempt to hire more black scholars, that is to correct something that is fundamentally wrong, and that is the exclusion of black students and professors from this university under apartheid. That, for me, is social justice, correcting what was wrong. Social justice means giving back land to people, the land that was stolen by colonialists, etc. Social justice is about doing right

The soft revolution 13

in relation to the past. Transformation, on the other hand, is about shaping the future. For me, it means that even though I might get more black scholars, if they still think like conservative scholars or they're still stuck in the past in terms of their own training, that's not transformation. It's important to have them here, but transformation means changing the way of *thinking*.

I was absolutely surprised when I discovered that St. Paul and I are in agreement here because the word transformation that he uses in Romans 12:2 is to be transformed in the renewing of your mind, which in Greek, where the word comes from, means metamorphosis. I make a distinction between simply correcting the past and then correcting the future, if you will, through a different kind of thinking. For me, social justice, whether in society broadly or in education, is about making amends for what went wrong in the past.

JA: You see both of these things being equally necessary at the same time?

JJ: Yeah. There's a bit of a Venn diagram here, an overlapping Venn diagram, because you can't really completely extract transformation issues from social justice. They overlap, but they're not the same; they're not identical because these words have a socially connected meaning, I'm not sure I'd put it in exactly that way if I was in another country. One of the reasons that some of our most dysfunctional provincial governments are in Mpumalanga and Limpopo provinces is quite simply because we took bad black people from the homeland governments under apartheid and assumed that when you take in more black people, you also take in progressively future-looking comrades. Nonsense! You're taking in the very people that benefitted from, fed off, and became part of the apartheid bureaucracy in the context of the homelands. Now, you might still make an argument you need to bring those persons into government at all levels because of the injustices of the past. But that does not mean that you have a transformed cadre. That's a very different kind of proposition.

JA: How does this understanding, your understanding of social justice and transformation in this case, inform your conception and practice of leadership? What does that look like? How does that translate in terms of how you think about and practice leadership?

JJ: When I think about social justice, I think about everybody who's been excluded from the university. Let me just take that as my unit of reflection in the past. People who are gay, people who were Catholic and Jewish, anybody who was not Afrikaans, Dutch, Calvinist, conformist, in relation to the apartheid state, anybody who didn't find a place here. People with disabilities who, even thought they might have believed certain things, were not allowed in or were allowed in without attending to their needs. People who are Muslim.

For me, social justice doesn't simply mean black people; social justice means all these dimensions of inequality, of poor treatment. People who rebelled and went to prison because they felt that they would not be conscripted into an unjust war. For me, justice isn't just race; justice is all these various

14 *Johnathan Jansen*

dimensions around which people were excluded, even though, obviously, race carried some primacy in the politics, particularly of apartheid. For me, whether it is putting up ramps for people in wheelchairs in every building, or whether it is creating alternative routes for access to students disadvantaged by the school system, as we do on our south campus, all of those things for me formed the collective of actions which hopefully satisfy the demands for social justice in our society.

JA: I know you have lots of stories, but I'm wondering what experiences, both personal and professional, inform your understanding and practice of leadership for social justice. Were there turning points, significant moments, significant individuals? What experiences did you have growing up, and as an adult, that had a powerful impact on shaping your understanding and desire to be a social justice leader?

JJ: I think it would be very difficult to lead without a road map of your own biography. Like today, when I spoke to my senior leaders, 25 of them, I recalled being excluded in so many different ways. And I said to them, "That is why we have to change. That is why." Even a simple thing that caused havoc the past three months at our university, which was simply a debate around changing the names of some of our student residences, because they're named after right-wing white supremacists. And what's a name? For me, it's important to remind people that these are divisive figures, that these are offensive figures in my memory, of how they operated. "Therefore, I hope we're all on the same page," I said to my colleagues, "when we change this stuff." Now of course, there's going to be noise outside; there's going to be right-wing reaction; there's going to be all kinds of preservationist attacks: That I can deal with. Are we on the same page as leaders of this institution?

I think your own biography, your own memory, your own experience often inform how you deal with those things. Secondly, I very much respond to demands. So if students come to me and say, "You know, Professor, every night I go to sleep in JBM [a residence hall named after JBM Hertzog, a former prime minister of South Africa from 1924–1939]. It's very difficult for me. I don't recognize this person except as an offensive figure in history. I have to respond to that. At the same time, my approach, as you probably know, is not to replace one set of offensive white nationalists with another set of offensive black nationalists.

Part of the approach is to sort of say, "Is there another way of doing this?" And as my colleagues proposed the other day, which I really liked: What if we name things in the context of our constitution's stated values? Here's something that I can work with, which on the one hand, is progressive, on the other hand, doesn't reinscribe nationalist or peculiar nationalist identities. By that, I don't mean there's a moral equivalence between somebody who fought in the struggle and somebody who fought against the struggle. But it does give you a more open, progressive terrain on which to shape the future of the university; it's not tied to individuals, etc.

The soft revolution 15

But having said that, because we have a commitment in our vision as a university to reconciliation, it's also the positive memories of people who stepped over, like Bram Fisher. When I dedicate my inaugural lecture to Bram Fisher, it is considered, it is thought about because here's a wonderful way of bringing into the present conciliator figures in our history who took a huge knock in standing up against injustice. That also, I think, plays a role, not just the bad side of that history but also the solidarity side of that history.

JA: On a personal note, I read somewhere that you were inspired by your high school Latin teacher, Paul Gallant. Could you talk about that?

JJ: I was a fairly average kid initially, I think, in school. I was always messing around, playing soccer all day and that kind of stuff. I didn't have people who told me I'm good at anything. It was just that way for so many of us young boys on the Cape Flats in those days. And here comes a teacher, and the first person ever to single me out and sort of say to me in a school break while I was playing soccer, he said to me: "You always pretend that you know nothing, but I think you're really smart. You're hiding your potential, that kind of thing." I didn't even have shoes on that day. But the impact that had on me was unbelievable because I knew he was a passionate teacher of Latin. I also knew that he didn't have to do that; it wasn't a school in which people were told they're good at anything. But that had such an impact on me. I remember from that day onwards opening up my books, doing my homework, going to the library, studying. Because I said, "Wow, somebody took an interest in me. Somebody said I'm smart – maybe test it out."

That's why I became a teacher initially because he had such a huge impact on me, the fact that you can as an individual change the lives, in my case, of tens of thousands of people from being a high school teacher, to having worked in poor communities, to having been a university leader at different levels at five universities. And I just realized you got an audience. Just before you came here, there must have been about six different students, black and white, who came in here looking for whatever, motivation, mentorship, money for this that or the other thing. So, yeah, Paul is a huge influence on my choices and my perspective.

JA: In your book, *We Need to Talk*, you have a couple of entries about your father. One you wrote on Father's Day, and you said that he was a very respected member of the community. People would come and ask him for advice, and he was a very important role model for you, especially in terms of education. You said he understood the value and joy of learning and education and somehow transmitted that to you as a young person. Could you talk about that?

JJ: You know, both my parents didn't finish high school because it wasn't necessary in those days, in some sense, so they went up to grade 10 and got a junior certificate, and it was a big deal in those days. But they skipped two years of high school because of, you know. But my father had a very deep

16 *Johnathan Jansen*

sense of the value of education, and he also had a very strong sense that your best is not good enough. Sometimes that would devastate me because I thought my best was good enough when I occasionally got that mark. He would always use the stock phrase, you know, "There's room for improvement," and that hit me between the eyes.

Years later I understood what he was saying; you can, in fact, do even better than that. And that stuck with me. I think parents only leave you with two or three things, not hundreds of things, two or three key values that you pick up along the way. And his contribution was that. He was also an extremely generous man; he gave away everything he had. We had nothing. The little we had he gave away to others who he thought were in great need. That's another value statement. That's why today I give away virtually everything I have to other people, because of him. Also always had his feet on the ground, was very self-deprecating, didn't think very much of people who were arrogant and full of themselves.

Hopefully, I've learned a lot about him from just trying to be humble, you know, in a context where everybody's telling you how wonderful you are. And I keep telling myself that's not true, that just because you got a certain set of accidental events happening in your life that gave you a foot up, doesn't mean you're anything special. I really do believe that, you know, that there are many smarter people than me at school, but I just got a break here than in any other place. One is grateful and always conscious of the fact that what you have is because of others. I'm very clear about that. But that I got from him as well.

JA: I know you grew up as a conservative evangelical Christian, and we'll get to that later. I know you were out of the country for a period of time from 1985 to 1991, then again when you did your Fulbright, and that you were influenced by Steve Biko's Black Consciousness Movement. Does your experience of the liberation struggle inform your understanding and practice of leadership for transformation and social justice?

JJ: One of the things I'm very conscious of is the enormous sacrifices that many people made for us to be free, and that is why my blood pressure goes up significantly when politicians undermine today the education of black kids, of poor kids. You must have read my diatribes against the 30% and 40% pass rates [on the matric, the high school graduation exam]. I find it so offensive on so many levels, because that's precisely the logic of apartheid. The logic of apartheid was white people can do math and science and all these wonderful things; black people can't. This is the same thing. The irony is that these are the very people who lost family members, who went into exile, who spent time in prison, who got beaten up because they believed we could have a more just society.

Every weekend I buy another book; I just bought two or three books this weekend. I listen to the stories of Ben Turok in exile [he fled South Africa in the mid-1960s after serving three years in Pretoria Central Prison to avoid serving additional years in jail for heading a sabotage unit of *Umkhonto we Sizwe*, the armed wing of the ANC, and lived in Kenya, Tanzania, England, and Zambia for the next 25 years], for example, of the new book on Nat Nakassa, sent on a one-way ticket out of South Africa and jumped to his death in New York City because he realized he was not accepted in the U.S. because of the so-called communist scare. But he couldn't go back home during apartheid, so he kills himself. I say to myself, "Wait a minute: These people made these sacrifices not so that we can vote, but so that we can lead a more decent life." That stuff is always prominent in my mind when I fight for a particular measure in education to raise up the lower end.

JA: Now, I understand your position on racial categories, that you abhor them, you reject them, you don't want anything to do with them, and as a young person you didn't like being labeled as a colored person. But you still grew up in an apartheid society and were treated in a certain way based on other people's perceptions of your racialized identity. In that context, does your racial assignment affect your understanding and practice of leadership?

JJ: Yes and no. On the one hand, I have a Biko Black Consciousness understanding. If you're going to pigeonhole me, call me black, by which Biko and that generation meant oppressed people, and interestingly, that could include white people. I remember the day when people said Cheeky Watson was black. Cheeky Watson was trying to do black rugby as a white man in the Eastern Cape at great risk to his life and his family's life. Of course, it meant black people, but it wasn't strictly speaking about color. It was about the *consciousness* of being oppressed.

Of course, in that sense, it definitely fills my desire for justice and for equality for all our people. But I'm also very conscious, and was always conscious of the fact, ever since I read Dan O'Meara's book, *Volkskapitalisme* (1983), that apartheid wasn't just a racially oppressive system; it was a class system, it was a capitalist system. Therefore, there were always poor whites. We saw them working as ticketing agents on the trains, on the black trains in the Cape Flats. You know that the only way this guy's got a job is because he is white. You knew it because you had more brains than him. You knew he got a job because he's white, and therefore the risks for him and those guys was much higher than for the middle-class Afrikaans person.

Both those things drive me. When I unashamedly make available bursaries [scholarships] and I make it public, to poor white Afrikaans kids, I'm unapologetic about it because it's the right thing to do – justice here also in terms of social class. On the one hand, yes, that understanding of being black in the broader sense drives me, of being colored. I don't ever figure that into my calculus with respect to social justice; black is enough. Secondly, at the same time I'm conscious of the fact that this is becoming a burden, and that we are reinscribing in the postapartheid youth the very categories we fought against. I am saying now, "Let's bring the best minds in the country together to think of new ways of dealing with inequality."

18 *Johnathan Jansen*

In the U.S. today, what does it mean to be black? It is so ridiculous, especially when you look at a place like New York City, where so many of the black people there, first of all, didn't come as slaves. Secondly, many of them are from interracial families: Barak Obama. What does it mean to insist that you're one thing, when you're in fact many things? Like the guy running for Congress [the U.S. Senate] who's the black Native American from Oklahoma [T.W. Shannon]. It's a fascinating story in the *New York Times* this last week that I quite enjoyed. I'm also conscious of the fact that we're playing games here with identities that are shifting so fast in a globalized world that we need to find other measures of inequality rather than these crude racial categories.

JA: I know that you've been heavily influenced by the work of Neville Alexander, who also opposed reinscribing racial categories.

JJ: Absolutely. At some point I felt we were the only two against this stuff.

JA: I want to double back just a second. In your book, *We Need to Act*, you talk about your experiences as an undergraduate at the University of the Western Cape and how it could take you up to four hours to get from the Cape Flats area to Bellville to go to school. You talked about how difficult that was: You'd get home at eight o'clock, leave the next morning at four o'clock, etc. You tell the story of being chased out of a chemistry class for being two minutes late, which was due to the fact that the bus broke down on the way to Bellville. This cruelty by the professor led you to sit outside of the first-year lecture room sobbing and to buy a newspaper to look for a job. Later you stood up to the chemistry professor and said, "You can fail me, but you cannot break me." This image of you sitting outside that classroom is burned into my mind's eye. It's just a heartbreaking image. You struggle four hours to get there, the bus breaks down, you're two minutes late, and this racist white professor throws you out of the classroom.

I think I'm jumping ahead here, but I'm going to ask this question now anyway. Ever since I read that, it's sort of been sitting with me. When I was putting together these questions, it suddenly came back to me, and I went through all the stuff I've been reading and finally tracked it down because it was a very powerful image. I'm wondering what enabled you to continue under those circumstances. What were the personal and social resources that you were able to draw on? What's the basis of your resilience in a situation like that? Did that incident inform your understanding and practice of leadership for transformation and social justice?

JJ: Look, if I think back to that particular episode, it's quite devastating. I didn't feel, to be honest with you, at that point, that I had any resources to go back on. I didn't feel there was anything I could do. My parents were poor; they didn't have money to send me to university. I was dependent on a friend, or uncle, and so on, that might give you 20 rand in those days to register and that kind of thing. I didn't feel, at least consciously, that there were resources to draw on; there weren't actually.

The soft revolution   19

Next I went to look for a job. I bought *The Cape Herald*, looked for a job, and got one at Anchor East, and that didn't last very long. Then something quite remarkable happened. There were also problems at home at that point, I remember, domestic problems. I remember an uncle of mine coming and saying, "Jump in the car. I'm taking you back to campus, to university in Bellville." He had a car. I remember him driving me, and talking to me and encouraging me, and saying, "Your mother asked me to do this because you shouldn't give up." So I went back. I am quite convinced if he wasn't there, if he did not drive me back that day, I am convinced I would be either working in a factory or selling newspapers or fish or whatever I was doing on the holidays in those days.

The lesson I draw is that I have brought to our campus many young people who come to study here from the Western Cape, from Steenberg, where I lived, from Nyanga and Masiphumelele, which were African townships around Cape Town. They're here a year, and I pay for them fully, but that's the easy part. The difficult part is I watch them like a hawk because I know they're going to go through what I went through, perhaps not blunt racism, like I did – like last night, at 11 o'clock one of them being at the hospital. Fortunately, I had a young colleague who took him there and updated me. I have to keep telling him, "don't go back to Nyanga. Stay with the program. Just get your degree." I'm doing to him exactly what this uncle did, which is, "I know this is a risky time. You can fall. You get rejected." Yet another chemistry test, yet another psychology test, yet another this, and then I get 40% and not 60%. A middle-class kid has resources to draw on, bounces back much more easily; a poor kid doesn't.

And then you need these multiple support structures, like my dear colleague who took him without me knowing to hospital, to a terrible public hospital at 11 o'clock at night. If she wasn't there, I'm sure he'd jump on the bus and say, "That's it." I picked up from that that you have a spiderweb of support structures that are very fragile, but necessary, to keep you staying on the road, as it were, towards the degree. That's why our dropout rate is so high in South Africa, very high. It's because a lot of poor kids just give up. Because I can relate to that, I try as far as I can to be part of that spiderweb of support, just the netting to catch you. It's very important.

JA: It's amazing how a simple twist of fate, how one intervention, can make all the difference. Because I've heard you speak many times, and I've read a lot of your work, I know that your practice is informed by your religious beliefs and that you grew up as a conservative evangelical Christian. How have your religious beliefs informed your understanding and practice of leadership for transformation and social justice?

JJ: It's a wonderful foundation on which to build your life. I'm the biggest critic of conservative evangelicalism, both in South Africa and the United States, because it hurt me in many ways as well, but it also gave me enormous structure, like a moral code. I'm not saying I always stuck to the

20 *Johnathan Jansen*

code, but there was this moral code, like respect your brother and sister, love those who hate you – simple stuff, you know, without which I don't know where this teacher would have come from. You know, protect yourself against harm, respect your parents. That stuff, to me, is so fundamental in the way we've raised our children and in the way we try to raise ourselves. I am very conscious of the positive aspects of conservative evangelical training, if you will, in my life. But I'm also very wide-awake to its horrors. One of its horrors is its exclusivism. One of its horrors is its negativity towards, for example, the Muslim faith, the Jewish faith, anybody else who disagreed with you. That was absolutely horrible, and we rebelled against that as young people; as we started to get our own minds in the church, we rebelled. That's why many of us left the church, if not always its values, which we kept; we left the church.

I made a big speech this morning to my senior colleagues. I said, "Did you realize that we just had a breakfast here, and there were Muslim colleagues, and you had bacon on the table? Do you understand? I've talked about this for four years, and you still don't get it right." Their heads would go down, and I know I have to keep pushing the issue – that it's so difficult to get a Muslim prayer room here – but there's 500 places you can pray as a Christian.

I pushed that stuff, just today, in fact, very hard, and I will make sure we win on those cases. My point is it guides me, but it also warns me about what not to do because I think that at the heart of being a Christian is being *generous*. As the president of Spellman [Dr. Beverly Daniel Tatum of Spellman College] put it so beautifully, she said, in all of our faiths, when she was here the other day, is the notion of welcoming the stranger. Isn't that beautiful? Welcoming the stranger – it's true of Islam. If you forget the fundamentalist readings of all these texts, it's about welcoming the stranger. We don't do that in conservative evangelicalism very well, and I think it's fundamental.

JA: In your inaugural speech at UFS you said, "I'm glad to lead because I am being led. I can forgive because I am forgiven." What does that mean to you?

JJ: Well, it does mean to me that in my spiritual experience, I'm so conscious of the fact that God forgave me for all this stuff, not just what I did but the person I was. And I remember very clearly how my life changed by making that commitment, again, in the context of conservative evangelical faith. I am very deeply grateful for that experience. Because I could see that all my friends around me didn't have those anchors and went their own ways and created chaos in their lives. I think once you've been forgiven, once you have this sense of being forgiven by the divine, you have a duty, in fact, to be able to forgive those who hurt you. That, it turns out, at a university like the Free State is, at least in precept, understood by everyone.

In practice, we're a very vengeful society. The only one that's more vengeful I think is your society [the U.S.]. I still can't believe you hang people, shoot people, put chemicals, experiment with drugs, and so forth. I think fundamental to the Christian faith ought to be this understanding of you're

The soft revolution 21

forgiven, you've got a second lease on life, you have been looked over where you should have been judged. That's what it means.

As I said, my own Christian faith has evolved from that very narrow literalist understanding, a fundamentalist understanding, to something that I hope is a lot more inclusive, less judgmental, etc. And conscious, also then, of being led – I'm so aware of that. It's very difficult to explain to somebody who doesn't believe all this stuff about the spiritual world. I'm very conscious of the fact, over and over and over again, that I am not acting on my own, that I am being guided by precepts deep in my head and my heart, that there are tracks behind me that I walk in into the future. And because of that sense of not being an individual acting out his own ego, it is possible for me to lead. I would feel very nervous as a leader, very unsure, if I didn't have a sense of security in being lifted as a leader myself.

Just to give you a quick sense – just before you came, I think, there was a student who came in. She stood over there, and she said, "Do you mind if I gave you a hug?" I said, "Yeah, OK." That to me is a spiritual experience; it's not material. It's a kid that says, "I just want to connect with you." For me, that sense of connection is spiritual, and I can lead because she just led me in that moment. The students who came here, three of them just came and said, "We'd just like to give you this rose to say thank you to you." This day alone was packed with people like that. So you lead because you've been led. It's very difficult to explain what that does, the confidence you get, but also the guidance you get from people who connect here on a spiritual level.

JA: Do you have a sense of obligation or responsibility to be a leader? I mean, where does it come from?

JJ: I don't ever think that, in my case, you're conscious that you're a leader. I remember when I first became aware of this thing, that people say, "Oh you're a leader," which was recent, five or 10 years ago. I went back to Cape Flats, and I went to talk to friends that went to school with me. I said, "Everybody says I'm a leader," but what was I really like? And I said, "Tell me something. What was I like at school? All I know is that I had a lot of fun with you guys." They said, "Do you remember you were the captain of the under 13C soccer team?" I said, "Yeah," then slowly sort of realized that somewhere there were things happening to you that sort of pushed you into leadership and that you led because you enjoyed it. But you didn't think of it as leadership. You just thought, "Hey, let's organize this team to play soccer." And so on the reflection only, you become aware of the fact that you were doing leadership without having a vocabulary for it, or without having a consciousness about it, and that you actually quite enjoyed it.

I think that's probably true for a lot of the things I've done. Of course, as you get older you become more aware of it; I suppose. But I still don't think of myself as a leader. I still don't think of myself as a really good leader. I am so conscious of the fact that my leadership is deeply influenced by co-leadership. Right now, as we sit here, I have four or five vice rectors

22 Johnathan Jansen

running the university, which is why I can talk to you. I don't have this inflated sense of the big man theory of leadership. That's such nonsense because you colead, really, in the best of times.

JA: That goes back to something that you said that I was curious to have you talk about. I'm curious about what you mean by brokenness. What does it mean that you have accepted and made peace with your own brokenness? What does it mean to be vulnerable and aware of your own brokenness, and why is this important?

JJ: This is absolutely crucial to me and mind-boggling intellectually and fulfilling personally. And that is the notion, the resignation, early on, that you are not really good at what you do. This is paradoxical in so many ways, right, because the South African sense of leadership, the global sense of leadership, the American sense of leadership, is the Jack Welsh model [the former CEO of General Electric]. That's rubbish. I like the notion of, and it works for me, and it's true that when you lead, what makes you strong is your sense of vulnerability, your sense of weakness, your sense of dependency on others, your sense of making bad decisions, your sense of facing a crisis and being uncertain, your sense of getting angry when things go wrong.

I don't regard that as necessarily fatal. I think that is a very important way of understanding authentic leadership in a very divided community. I will never go out, and if it happens, I would be very ashamed of myself. I never go out and say, "I think I know the six steps to this." It's rubbish. You don't because too often, you say to yourself, "My goodness, what do I do next? What do I do now?" So I'm aware of that brokenness. I'm aware of the fact that even with my best intentions, I might hurt a colleague. I'm aware of the fact that you cannot have my biography and not at some point have hated people, and I'm very ashamed of that, but I hated white people for a long time because of what happened to us.

I suppose the opposite of that is I don't come into leadership with a sense of self-righteousness, a sense of being on the good side, and there's the bad side. I come in more with a sense of being extremely vulnerable to my own past and uncertain of our own future, and that enables me to be confident. I don't know if that paradox makes any sense. I would be nervous if I felt so sure of everything. And that is something I genuinely mean because I see too many friends of mine who are leaders who are so sure of themselves, who have never said sorry, who have never apologized. I apologize regularly.

JA: I saw you apologize in public when I attended a university assembly. I've seen you do that, in public, apologize for things that you may have done: I may have hurt you; I may have overlooked you or whatever.

JJ: I don't know how that could not be true. I often say sorry to my children, which I know my parents, not because they were bad parents – they weren't – because it wasn't in their upbringing to say that. I find a lot of fulfillment in being able just to be real with regard to one's own weaknesses.

JA: At the end of a video of interviews with you (*Transformational Leadership*, n.d.), you say, "Leadership cannot be perfect, but it must be an honest leadership about what we can do and what we can't." What are some of the things that transformational leaders cannot do?

JJ: First of all, as a transformational leader, you cannot change people who do not want to be changed. Now that's very difficult because of the sort of sweeping sense we have, particularly in the evangelical community. You don't just look after the 99 sheep; you go after that one sheep until you find it. It's a really powerful thing. But the truth is a transformational leader cannot impose transformation, you know; it has to be something that people accept or not. You can create, as far as you can, the conditions that promote acceptance of human ideals like forgiveness and so forth, but you can't actually push people there. That's something that was hard for me initially to accept and understand; that you can't do. It means you remember that beautiful prayer: Help me understand what I can change, what I can't change, and the difference. That's very powerful stuff.

Secondly, you can't as a transformational leader really impose your own particular view of what is right and wrong on people. You really have to draw on the best that is available to you through the biographies of groups of people. The other day I heard a phrase that completely blew me away in this respect. If you said to me, "What was the life-changing moment for this year," it was this. The president of Ireland had invited Queen Elizabeth to Ireland. If you know anything about the conflict in that part of the world, these are centuries-old conflicts. Then Queen Elizabeth invited the president of Ireland. She then makes a speech welcoming him and saying all these important things about our peoples and our histories, you know, the normal thing. Then he gets up, and I'll never forget what he said, that we might be helped to embrace the better versions of ourselves; I mean, that blew me away. You know there's a bad version of yourself, right!

Part of leadership, if I interpret what he said, is to embrace the better version of ourselves because we have a choice here. I think what a leader has to do, a transformational leader, is to recognize that better version and understand there's another version that you simply have to leave at bay. Part of the storytelling as a leader, and I'm quite amazed at how much you've picked up through various collections of things about my own work, is to constantly remind people of the better versions of themselves; that is your role as a leader. Because I could make a long story about the Afrikaner and history and so forth, but you have to keep leaning back to the better versions of ourselves. A transformational leader cannot impose the whole story.

JA: How do you connect with the better side?

JJ: Because it's available to us. Just today, where you sit, sat several people who came to see me about various things, one of which was my suggestion, in fact it was more, that we no longer continue to have these old apartheid names. One of the colleagues said, "But then what do we draw on?" And I said, "It's

24   *Johnathan Jansen*

very easy: Bram Fisher. Here's a better version of ourselves as Afrikaners; he's not here, but here's a better version of ourselves. You don't have to remind me that Peter Mokaba [known for the 'kill the Boer, kill the farmer' slogan] was a horrible racist hack, an ANC struggle hero. But there's a better version in Nelson Mandela." We discussed that. That's, I think, what you do, is recognizing there are some bad stories out there; let's draw on the good stories as we embrace the future. That, I think, is the role of a leader.

JA: What are the greatest personal and institutional challenges to practicing leadership for social justice in higher education but specifically here at UFS?

JJ: I think one of the biggest challenges is finding a way of making social justice real in the lives of the people most affected. At a very basic level, how do you get enough money into the institutions so that every poor kid, and particularly every poor black kid, can get through the three or four years of study without too much stress? That's a *huge* challenge. I grapple with that daily – so many smart talented young people, but they don't have the money.

Our government overpromises, and in an election year in both our countries, people go over the top. At the end of the day, you still have to get that kid money to study. Until the whole system changes for selection and finance, I'm stuck in trying to keep a university financially stable and at the same time academically accessible. That's a huge challenge at the heart of what we do. So I spend a lot of time on the road. A lot of books that I write, I give the royalties back.

JA: I know you gave part of your first year's salary back when you became vice chancellor and rector.

JJ: You give chunks of what you earn back to the university all the time. That, for me, is the big thing. I was in the top of an open bus going into one of the townships the other day, and the white Dutch Reformed minister, a very progressive guy actually, he looked at me, watching me all the time as we drove through the township handing out food parcels and that kind of thing. He said to me, "What enters your mind when you see all of these shacks and so on, and the promise we made, a solemn promise to these young people, to these communities, that we will serve them better after apartheid?" That's my nightmare. We made a promise; now how do we live, those of us who have the means and the opportunity to lead? How do you live up to that promise? If I work 20 hours a day, it's because I am so concerned that we meet the terms of the contract.

JA: You've talked about this a lot in your writings. It's not only unjust; it's a huge waste of talent and intellectual capacity and everything the country needs to develop and prosper. I know you encounter resistance to your leadership; I've seen it all over, everywhere. What kind of resistance do you encounter, and how is your response to this resistance informed by your understanding of leadership for transformation and social justice?

JJ: I think when you're a leader of a university in the center of the country, you're going to have problems in a historically white university, in an Afrikaans university. You're going to have problems because you'll be attacked no matter what you do from both extremes – both from the black nationalist extreme that believe that the only way of getting justice is to supplant white presence with black domination. That, I'm dead set against. You also get huge resistance, as I do daily, from the white right, who believe that any presence of black people here is the end of their own livelihoods, their own white nationalist projects, etc. In some ways, early on I made my peace with the fact that you're going to get resistance; it sort of ebbs and flows.

There will be particular weeks when it's really tough on my staff, my secretary, myself, and my family, in which you get death threats and in which you get letters that I can't believe any human being can write – and Twitter responses and so forth. But that's on the extreme. The way I deal with that is to say it's the extreme, is to remind myself that the majority of people on this campus, in this country, black and white, rich and poor, are actually not like that. That's factually true, and it's particularly true on our campus now compared to, let's say, six or seven years ago when every issue divided people clean into black and white. When we had that horrible incident on campus where two guys allegedly knocked over another guy, and the two happened to be white, the other one black [A black student alleged that two white students tried to run him over with a vehicle while he walking on the campus and then assaulted him when he confronted them at a nearby residence hall. The white students were acquitted of all charges by the Bloemfontein Regional Court and the South African Human Rights Commission], the march that happened was an interracial march, black and white together saying, "That is not us." That gave me such a relief. If that was just a black crowd showing up, I would have considered resigning because it means I did nothing here. But the fact that black and white showed up saying, "That is not us," that I had hundreds of letters of support saying that is not the Human Project we fight for.

Then you've got to be realistic. As I often say to myself, you can't have three centuries of colonialism and apartheid and expect everybody to be angels: You're mad. I live with the fact that, for a long time to come in our country, and even perhaps on this campus, you are going to have those voices on the side. The trick for leadership is to keep them on the side, to keep them marginalized within the broader project. But, again, it's unrealistic to expect everybody to be singing angelic songs in unison; we've been divided for too long for that to happen.

The closest analogy, actually, to the University of the Free State is actually the University of Mississippi [located in a former Confederate state in the Deep South of the U.S.]. They have exactly the same issues, having been baptized in the language of slavery, and segregation, and Jim Crow [a system of legalized racial segregation established after the Civil War and Reconstruction in former slaveholding states in the South], and so on. Every now and again they have a big incident [a noose was hung around the neck of a statue of James Meredith on the campus, a black student who racially integrated the University of Mississippi in 1962]. If you change the names of the leadership

26   *Johnathan Jansen*

there, you just change the event, it's exactly the same here. That's a function of history. A key, as I said, for leadership is how do you lead out of that, progressively, by making sure that the middle remains deracialized, or in South African terminology, nonracial. You saw the open letter I wrote after that; it's about the consensus that sticks, and then you've done your job.

JA: You accept the reality that there are going to be judicial responses to these things, but that's not your approach. Your approach is not to sort of push it off on the judicial system and let them solve, or attempt to solve, the problem. As I understand it, and correct me if I'm wrong, you really see it as a cultural issue, an issue of the institutional culture of the university. You want to change the culture of the university, and judicial solutions do not do that, so you take the more difficult road of trying to bring people together.

JJ: In all of these cases that we've had, all of them, whether it's black against white or white against black, in all of these cases, we have to, just as a matter of good governance, initially refer these things to disciplinary and legal processes. But almost simultaneously, with the institute [Institute for Reconciliation and Social Justice] and with some other senior colleagues, we try to see where there is another way. Where people are willing to do that, we solve most of the problems – not all of them. It doesn't happen immediately. Even with Reitz, you needed months to go by, and people's hurt and anger, and it just happened to get over the worst of that. Then you start talking and say, "Do you think there's an opportunity here just to talk about this?" We're doing that now with one of the bad cases. We know from experience that it doesn't happen in a linear way. It's back and forth and back and forth, but eventually people realize that in the long term, the grievances are never solved simply by a judge putting down his hammer on the case. It's solved through human dialogue, and I learned to be patient about that.

JA: I know you've answered this many times, and you partially addressed it already. What keeps you going in the face of resistance to your leadership? You've talked about people coming out and supporting you and the consensus, but what gets you through the tough times?

JJ: I think, first of all, a very deep sense of knowing right from wrong. For me, I would be much more uncertain, much more panicky, if I didn't know the difference between right and wrong on almost all of these issues. By the time I've taken a decision I know, like with the Reitz thing, I knew that was the right way to go, and I knew there'd be flack, but I also knew we'd come out tops afterward. On almost all of these issues, for me, even though there's temporary hurt and pain, I know there's long-term gain. Having a clear sense of that, in almost any case, helps me enormously.

I do doubt myself. I do ask myself tough questions. I am uncertain at points, but at the root your value system is clear. If you are going to lay your hands on a woman, as one of my male students, I don't have to think about it; I really don't have to think about it. I just know this is right, to act against you; so that helps me enormously. The second issue is I have an enormous support network, not just in South Africa but internationally. I just got this huge set of things that just arrived from the University of California. You get a lot of things like that every day. Not that kind of thing, but I mean of encouragement, of the kid that says can I give you a hug; the kid who comes to play; the kid who dropped the rose. Just today itself is a wonderful example of how you are encouraged. The noise dims to a large extent when there is so much support, so much encouragement, so much love in the middle of a crisis.

Number three, I've learned a lot better now than before to know that my ability to serve the university well depends on taking out time to be with yourself. I just spent two weeks in Cape Town alone in a house with my own readings and my own reflections and my own thoughts, and when I come back, I'm ready to take on the world again. You see this in the two great books on women's leadership that have just emerged, *Thrive* (2014) by Arianna Huffington and *Lean In* (2013) by Sheryl Sandberg. Both of those books are about how you create spaces for your own humanity, your own emotional health, your own spiritual health, failing which, you will burn out, and you will not lead well.

I've become better at that, I think. Then it helps that your spouse has a strong understanding of what you're about and what you're trying to do; she understands that you can't quit in the middle of a very important project. The last thing I wanted to say about that is I know I'm not here to lead the university of the Free State; that's the easy job. I know that what is at stake here is a much bigger national project, and that is establishing in central South Africa a university that really overcomes the worst features of our terrible history. To that extent, this is a very important project. I don't see it as managing the budgets, parking spaces, and all that – important as that is. I see this as part of a much *bigger* picture. If you keep focusing big picture, small struggles, big picture, small struggles, you gain perspective on what you're doing. That is quite healthy, I think.

JA: I know the concept of transformation has a history in South Africa, and that people often mean different things by it, and that it's been used politically. You've talked a little about your conception of transformation. How does your understanding of transformation inform your conception and practice of leadership?

JJ: One of the first things about my understanding of transformation has really been the transformation of thinking, transformation of the mind, is to put in place across the institutional architecture things that shift minds in a different direction, in a more progressive direction. The core curriculum is fundamental, and therefore, as you would expect, some resistance to being able to say there's a new way of thinking around science, around humanities, around law and ethics, around history, the stuff I teach, etc. That is the transforming of the mind.

The F1 study abroad program is fundamental to our strategy to place students, while they're still first years, freshman, in a completely different

28 *Johnathan Jansen*

cultural context where they're challenged to recalibrate around their own measures of humanity. The 50 to 60 seminars in any given month, that would never have happened here, with people from all over the world, with completely different thinking, to which our students are exposed. The modeling of race relations through not speaking but showing in different ways. In almost everything I do I try to project, for the students' consumption, a model of how you can be that is not so narrowly racially confined, as is so much of their lives before they got here. That for me is how we try to enact it.

The assembly is a platform for saying and reminding: This is what we stand for. Every meeting today, last week Thursday with the council meeting, I say, "I just want to remind all of you as leaders what we stand for just in case you don't know yet." Those are important opportunities. Transformation for me means shifting the mind in a way. I think most people by now trust me. They might not always agree with me, but they trust me. That this is necessary, not just to believe in but to try to enact in a way that is fair.

JA: I've read your work on political symbolism, and that is clearly present and up front in all the public events that I've seen. It's been very clear that that's important to you.

JJ: Oh, for sure, and my mentor. I forgot my own mentor Chabani Manganyi [N. Chabani Manganyi is a professor at the University of Pretoria]. If he says anything to me, he reminds me all the time: Symbols matter.

JA: I was present at the Open Day extravaganza yesterday [a welcoming event for new and prospective students and their families]. It was really amazing for everyone. First of all, the place was packed; lots of high school students were there and lots of white folks. I was amazed at how many parents and families came. I thought, "This is a great testament to where the university is now and where it wants to go."

JJ: Yeah, for sure.

JA: Is there anything we haven't discussed that you would like to add? Anything we've not talked about or overlooked?

JJ: No. I don't often get a chance to reflect on what I do in conversation with a senior scholar. I quite enjoy it, just to sort of see: Am I making sense in my own leadership? Thank you very much. Did you ever read that piece I wrote [*King James, Princess Alice, and the Ironed Hair: A Tribute to Stephen Bantu Biko*] in the book on Biko (Jansen, 2007)? That is a really nice summary as well of some developments, but you've captured the essence.

Significance and implications

In his remarks, Professor Jansen does precisely what he urges others to do: to think differently, in this case about how to conceptualize and practice educational leadership. He urges us to reject corporate models of leadership in favor of an approach that emphasizes the importance of self-knowledge, uncertainty, vulnerability, humility, and acting with moral courage.

Professor Jansen rejects the notion of the great man or woman, of the solitary and decisive leader, in favor of a concept of leadership that acknowledges the brokenness of leaders, the inevitably that they will make mistakes, and the reality that they cannot lead by themselves. His notion of leadership, which is rooted in a strong moral sense of what is right and wrong and in deeply held religious convictions, can inform how educational leaders think about themselves as leaders and the nature and aims of their leadership.

References

Gobodo-Madikizela, P. (Interviewer). (n.d.). *Transformational leadership: Jonathan Jansen* [Video]. Bloemfontein: University of the Free State.

Huffington, A. (2014). *Thrive: The third metric to redefining success and creating a life of well-being, wisdom, and wonder*. New York: Harmony Books.

Jansen, J. (2007). King James, Princess Alice, and the ironed hair: A tribute to Stephen Bantu Biko. In C. Van Wyk (Ed.), *We write what we like* (pp. 123–132). Johannesburg: Wits University Press.

Jansen, J. (2009). *Knowledge in the blood*. Stanford: Stanford University Press.

Jansen, J. (2011). *We need to talk*. Johannesburg: Bookstorm & Pan MacMillan.

Jansen, J. (2013). *We need to act*. Johannesburg: Bookstorm & Pan MacMillan.

O'meara, D. (1983). *Volkskapitalisme: Class, capital and ideology in the development of Afrikaner nationalism, 1934–1948*. Cambridge: Cambridge University Press.

Sandberg, S. (2013). *Lean in: Women, work, and the will to lead*. New York: Alfred A. Knopf.

3 The question of fairness
Creating opportunities to succeed

M.G. Sechaba Mahlomaholo

Professor Sechaba Mahlomaholo is senior research professor and dean of the Faculty of Education at the UFS. He is a devout Christian whose approach to leadership is strongly influenced by his religious faith and experience growing up in black townships in the eastern Free State province. After attending a secondary boarding school in QwaQwa, a former homeland or Bantustan (townships typically did not have secondary schools), Professor Mahlomaholo enrolled at the University of the North (also known as Turfloop), where he received a UED in education, a BA in education, and a BEd honors in special educational psychology in 1986. Professor Mahlomaholo went on to earn an MEd in counseling and consulting psychology from the Harvard University Graduate School of Education and a DEd in psychology of learning from the University of the Western Cape in 1998.

Professor Mahlomaholo has worked at six universities in South Africa in various capacities, including research professor, director of curriculum studies, director of research and postgraduate studies, head of the Professional Education Department, deputy dean, and senior lecturer and head of the Educational Psychology Department. In 2011 he became head of the School of Mathematics, Natural Sciences and Technology Education at the UFS.

Professor Mahlomaholo is an internationally recognized scholar who has served as editor and guest editor for a number of prominent journals and has been a keynote speaker and guest lecturer at universities in the United States, Russia, the UK, Denmark, and Canada. He has edited or coedited several books and published numerous journal articles and book chapters. Professor Mahlomaholo also collaborates with international colleagues on a number of projects, including the Global Network Project (Russia); the Post-Colonial Education Project (Trinidad and Tobago); the Intellectuals, Knowledge, and Power Project (Czech Republic); the Sustainable Education Project (Denmark); and the Discourse, Power, Resistance Project (the UK).

Professor Mahlomaholo practices what he calls 'invitational leadership,' which means that rather than using coercion or the threat of punitive sanctions to motivate faculty, he creates the conditions that make it possible for them to flourish. That is, rather than continually monitoring and pressuring faculty to increase their scholarly productivity, he nurtures their capabilities and provides opportunities for professional growth and development.

The question of fairness   31

Professor Mahlomaholo takes the same leadership approach is his work with postgraduate students. Given the long history of racial oppression and exploitation in South Africa, and the educational legacy of colonialism and apartheid, many students from previously marginalized and excluded groups have received inadequate preparation for university studies. However, rather than exclude them from the university, Professor Mahlomaholo seeks to give students opportunities to succeed by providing them with personal encouragement, academic support, and financial resources. That is, he seeks to ensure fairness and redress past injustices by providing students with the resources they need for academic success.

Professor Mahlomaholo also heads the project on Sustainable Learning Environments (SULE) at the UFS, which prepares postgraduate students to utilize participatory action and critical emancipatory research methods to address problems and improve the quality of public education in South Africa. Along with other faculty who participate in the project, he holds monthly meetings with a cohort of approximately 50 postgraduate students from around the Free State region to discuss research methods and assist students who are at various stages in their research. One of the key objectives of the SULE project is to create a cohort of young scholars who are committed to addressing problems in public education in conjunction with communities. Through SULE, Professor Mahlomaholo aims to develop a new generation of researchers who are committed to finding solutions to pressing issues in public education and to advancing equity and social justice rather than merely identifying problems.

To this end, the SULE project convenes an annual international colloquium on the Bloemfontein campus of the UFS that brings South African scholars together with colleagues from around the world. Postgraduate students are encouraged to present their work at the colloquium, where they have an opportunity to discuss and refine their research. For many young South African scholars, their participation in the SULE colloquium also provides them with their first opportunity to publish in a professional education journal.

Creating opportunities for colleagues and postgraduate students to succeed is at the heart of Professor Mahlomaholo's approach to leadership. For him, education should foster self-respect and respect for others and provide students, especially those from previously marginalized and excluded groups, with opportunities and resources for personal growth and academic success.

Professor Mahlomaholo (hereafter **SM**) began our conversation by discussing the core religious beliefs that underlie and provide an ethical foundation for his conception and practice of leadership for social justice.

SM: I should try to reflect on my understanding of social justice. It may not be very scientific, but this is just how I think about it: the question of fairness, fairness in your treatment of everybody. I should maybe indicate that I'm a Christian and attend church at least twice a month. I strongly believe that the Bible has a lot of wonderful things to dictate as to how we should conduct ourselves and relate to one another. My understanding, especially now of late, is that the whole Bible – I don't know how long in terms of the number of pages – I think it can be summarized in the Ten Commandments. Even further than that, I can't remember who said those words: Do unto others as you would like them to do unto you. That is a Christian thing, and I believe it's universal to every other religion and every other interrelationship amongst people. That seems to be the defining way of relating.

We don't do unto others because we're extremely altruistic. We do unto others because we firstly look at ourselves; what would we prefer other people do to us? That, for me, becomes the starting point of relating to other people. If I feel something would be particularly uncomfortable to other people, I really am very cautious and do that with great pain, I should say. That's why I honestly have been trying all along to avoid being in a leadership position or a management position because I know you have to sometimes make very difficult decisions like firing somebody, like reprimanding, like all those kinds of things. Personally, I don't like these things happening to me, so I really find it very hard to do unto other people.

My understanding of social justice is that I become the yardstick for measuring what to do to other people. If it is something I can have somebody do to me with ease, then I can do it with ease to other people: That's what drives me. I've read a few things on the definition of social justice that talk about fairness. The two things, for me, are relationships of respect to other people and, secondly, the distribution of privilege and resources, the equitable distribution of resources, and opportunities, and money. For me, these are the critical things, so when I talk about social justice, I'm understanding it in that respect. I'm understanding that creating opportunities for other people to succeed inasmuch as I like other people to do unto me. Those are the two things that inform my understanding and therefore my relationship, my interaction, and my actions in the end. I strongly believe in that. For me, those are very fundamental principles.

JA: So there's a human relational aspect and a material distributional aspect for you.

SM: Yes. That's how I have come to understand it. But underpinning that is: What is it that I'd love happening to other people? What I'd love other people to do to me is really what I want to do to other people. I'd love people to be respectful to me, to act respectfully. I am really very sensitive to very disrespectful conduct. I really feel this demeaning or undermining me in whatever manner. In the situation, either I respond very negatively or I withdraw or move away from the potentially hurtful situation. In everything that I do, I really try not to ultimately hurt anybody and actually to be proactive and create situations in which it is possible for another person to feel comfortable.

JA: By creating spaces, opportunities for other people?

SM: Yes. Because I'd love other people to do that for me. To some extent, I'm where I am because there were people who did that for me. I am eternally

The question of fairness 33

grateful and consciously aware that there were people who did many great things for me, in particular, as a person.

JA: I'd like to talk about some of those things, specifically about the experiences that inform your understanding and practice of leadership for social justice. What are those things that stand out in your experience, that have left a lasting imprint on you, that have led you to become the educational leader you are today? [Professor Mahlomaholo became dean of the Faculty of Education after this interview was conducted].

SM: I think one person that has had a very profound influence and impact on my life has been my father, who has passed on now. I've actually seen the very great sacrifices that he had gone to in order to see us get some little education. He never had the same privileges that he wanted to create for me and my sister. It has always been his lifetime objective; this is what he wanted to do throughout his life. Ever since I can remember, until he passed on, all the time he always put our interests above his. At times it would be at his own expense – but even in situations in which we were not there, you see. For some people, you do certain nice things because you want those people to see that, really, you are doing these nice things for them. But he would do that even in our absence. We only would discover, by the way, this is what this person had done for me, anonymously and without wanting to be glorified for that.

I might be digressing a little bit, but recently, about a month ago, I just had some informal conversation with my mother that my father actually said to her before I was born – because I was born at a time when many children were dying very young – at birth and so on. My father had told her that if I would die, he would also kill himself. He never said that to me. Nobody ever said anything for the 56 years that I've been alive. But I could see in his conduct all the time that it was a way of trying to protect, to create that space, not only for me and my sister but for many other people. That person has really had a very profound influence on my life.

But I've met many people, really, some of whom you know recently; maybe I can quote them. People like Milton [Dr. Molebatsi Nkoane, former head of the School of Educational Studies] made many sacrifices. That's why our friendship has become what it is. We have gone through very difficult circumstances, where sometimes, if it were some other people, it would have been easier for him to choose the other way of doing things, but he stood by our principles.

Not that we agreed on everything, but even this team that's growing, we faced so many insults, humiliations – many things that happened. But Milton stood up and protected that dream, at least because there was one other person that believed what we had in mind with that dream. All the time we talked about the dream and how it would materialize. That's one other person that taught me, that reinforced that question of fairness. You sometimes sacrifice your own things, your own interests, in order to protect another person. That consistently came through.

34   *M.G. Sechaba Mahlomaholo*

Maybe the last one that I can relate is coming here. You know, I worked so hard at Potchefstroom [the Potchefstroom campus of North West University], where I'd been working, and I really pushed a lot of boundaries believing that people would not look at my complexion but look at the work that I was doing. But in spite of all that, people would kick me in the teeth. The situation had gone so bad – I don't know how to describe that – but every time you were in a situation where you had to justify yourself, irrespective of how nicely you really tried to react, to relate to people.

When Dennis [Professor Dennis Francis, the former dean of the Faculty of Education] got here, I just told him that really I don't think I will survive. I don't know, the two and a half years that I stayed there, how did I manage to do that. Dennis went out of his way to make it possible for me to move out of that almost fatal – I'll call it that; that was how extreme the situation was. I think he did that against all odds. I don't think it was easy for him to convince whomever that maybe I could come and join the staff here. These were some of the things that were so profound in my life that every minute I think of that.

JA: Did you grow up in Ladybrand [a black township in the eastern Free State province]?

SM: How shall I put that? I didn't actually grow up in Ladybrand. My father was a teacher, and he would stay at a place for some short period of time and then move on to the other. During his time, being a teacher was very difficult, it also was dictated to by whether you were a member of the Dutch Reformed Church [a key institution of Afrikaner nationalism]. He wasn't one, but then ultimately he found that he had to join the church, but not because he really wanted to. He had to do that [to keep his job]. I've really never stayed in Ladybrand.

We stayed at all these other places, but that was his home. He also didn't stay there. I didn't even go to school there. By the time he went to stay in Ladybrand, I think this was in 1970, then I had to start high school, and there was no high school in Ladybrand [black townships typically did not have secondary schools] but in QwaQwa [one of ten homelands or Bantustans created for blacks under apartheid]. That's where I spent five years, coming home for a month, one and a half months. Really, I didn't grow up there. I can't say exactly where it is that I spent most of my time. Let me say that most of that time I spent in QwaQwa; that's where you'd find me when I was in high school.

Then when I completed high school, there was no university [in QwaQwa]. I had to go to what is now Polokwane [in Limpopo province], some 1,000 kilometers from Ladybrand. I could have easily come here [to the UFS], but I was not allowed to come to such [whites only] institutions. So I went there for another five years. Those are my homes. When I completed my studies, I spent a year in Ficksburg [a town in the eastern Free State province about 50 kilometers north of Ladybrand]. Then I went to QwaQwa because we were encouraged to go into those Bantustans. It was really not easy sometimes to find employment in places like Mangaung [a township near

The question of fairness 35

Bloemfontein in the Free State province], Bloemfontein, and so on. Those are the experiences. I don't know what it means to grow up in Ladybrand. I was always all over the place.

JA: You said that you were strongly influenced by your religious beliefs. What church do you belong to?

SM: I belong to the Methodist Church. I really find a home there in terms of the music, the Scriptures; in fact all these things are everywhere. But I really find comfort, maybe just because I'm used to the kind of singing, the kind of whatever.

JA: Was your family religious when you were growing up?

SM: Yes, my mother, my father, were religious.

JA: You haven't talked about your mother. What was her influence?

SM: My mother, she has influenced me a lot in terms of how I relate to women, I think because she was not as visible as my father was but even more powerful than my father. Most of the things that happened, it was because of her managing things from the background. Even today, she still does that. We hardly feel the absence of my father because she's still there to provide leadership. I don't know if it makes sense to you because I know in your practices it would be me having to take charge of my family only. But in ours, we really have that extended relationship where parents; they remain that forever.

JA: Yes, it is different here. In the United States we typically make a lot of distinctions between immediate and extended family, but here those distinctions kind of blur.

SM: Even with our white people here, at 18 their children have to go away, and when their parents are old, they don't stay with them. They have to go to old age homes: We don't do that. We stay with them, and it's actually an honor to have mature grown-up people with you all the time.

JA: How does your understanding of social justice, as relational and distributional, inform your experience and practice as a leader here at the UFS? How do you translate your understanding of social justice into everyday practice?

SM: I do exactly that: Do unto others as you would like them to do unto you. I've actually realized it's less stressful when people do things because they believe in what they are supposed to do rather than forcing and coercing them. This is one thing that has created problems for me. People would expect me to be angry and to force people to do things: I don't do that. But I try to make it desirable for people to do certain things. I've seen that working much better than people who do certain things because they are afraid.

Now the big issue in the Faculty [of Education] or the university is for people to publish, and normally what people would do is to force and threaten those who don't: I don't do that. I make it possible for those who don't publish to see that it's nice really to publish and that we do all kinds of things to support them. We have been fortunate; we share the same views as Professor Jita [Loyiso Jita is a professor in the School of Mathematics,

Natural Sciences and Technology Education], who is a wonderful person, who is able to generate a lot of money. He only arrived in 2011, but every year he has funding of over 1 million rand, last year over 3 million rand. He's a professor of physical science education. Last year, out of that number of millions he gave us 160 thousand rand for our school; that came in very handy for me. What I did was, especially with these younger people who have not published, I gave them 30 thousand rand each to say, "Here is the money; do research and publish. But we'll also fund your traveling internationally, but you must publish." In order to achieve that, then we have workshops to assist them to write, where we invite other people to come and do that. There is no complaint to say, "We don't have this, we don't have that," because it has become possible for them to do so.

We won this tender with the North West government. I wrote a proposal in which we won about 900 thousand rand [approximately 64 thousand U.S. dollars at the time]. After I paid all our costs, we might be left with about 400 thousand rand, which I'm going to use to support these guys to do their work because we only get 30 thousand rand from the university for 10 people; it's not possible to do many of the things. I'm trying to say, all these things, I see them. I believe more in invitation than in coercion because I know coercion is strenuous; I would not be able to do that. I can't just be looking after these 10 people, what they do. I don't have time for that because then I will forget to live myself. I am busy already without having to look after them. But then, if we agree on certain outcomes, it's just to check that. Whether they come to work or not, it doesn't matter. But I know that they are there. They also see, they also feel, the energy that we just have to do the right thing; that's all.

JA: You trust them to do the right thing.

SM: Yes. I think that is correct. I've seen that if you trust people to do the right things, you don't have to police them, but it takes time. They have to see me doing certain things, that I am also still at work after half past four, then they will want to do that too.

Yesterday we were celebrating in our school here. When I joined the school, the publication output was less than one, and last year we had 14. We had promised the dean that we'd do seven units, but we did 14. Some of the people who published had never published before. It has been that consistent support and recognition. You know, sometimes it's just to tell a person that you've done well;, it changes their perception around themselves and what they can do. If you do that consistently, not only in words, but also in actions, it is motivating. I strongly believe more in invitational leadership rather than in pushing people, which is costly, not in terms of money; but emotionally it's taxing, and you have to be behind this person pushing all the time forever. Imagine you have to do that to 14 people. I'd really be very busy!

That was reinforced by my training in education, where I have ultimately realized that everybody is capable of anything and everything, only if we had the patience to take this person by the hand up to the extent where he or she can fly. I've actually seen that happening in many instances, if you believe and trust in people. People have done that to me. Personally, I've gone through a couple of phases in life where I've long been in the social dustbin, but there were people who believed; I just needed support and help. Ultimately, I've become what I've become, which I'm really very happy. Even if I begin with different circumstances in life, I still think I'll do the same thing I'm doing now. I strongly believe in that, and I've seen that work on many occasions.

JA: Your style is invitational, but it's not just an invitation; it's an invitation that comes along with support, with both research support and financial support.

SM: Yes, that is critical. I have also seen that with our students. To get one PhD through is not easy. We interact with these people so that even when we are not there with them, they still feel like we are there. They don't want to disappoint. I think that's the main thing; they don't want to disappoint us. They have to do extra things, like be at work on Saturdays, be at work over December [during the summer holiday]. Others didn't even go away; that's the level of commitment. If they were afraid that I would do certain things, I doubt if they would have come to that life.

This is what I'd like people to do for me, which I've been trying to tell people. Really, I don't like somebody breathing down my neck; it makes you not want to do that. Give a space and support, then I can explore and find even better ways of doing what I'm supposed to do. Everybody has the minimum objectives that they have to reach, then occasionally we check how far we are. At the beginning of the year, each person has to come up with what we call a wish list: I want to go to this conference, one international and at least one local one; I want to publish one article; I want to do this. Every month we just get a report from them: How far are you with that? What could be the challenges? Last year it was seven articles. I think we did more than that; I think we did 12 or 13 in our school, which is unheard of. Our school was producing not even one, but now there are 10 of us. If we produce 13, then it means we are even higher than the national average.

We have clear systems; it's not about fear, honestly. Somebody I never even thought, someone who was, how shall I put that, a right-wing conservative Afrikaner, came to me to say he wants to work with me and that we write articles together: I said, "No, that's fine." Then he said he has to do something for me, so that he can do that for me, then I agreed. He will teach me technology, how to use the iPad, and I'll teach him. We agreed, every week we are meeting for mutual support. People didn't want to come here, this school biting them. I ignore that. It becomes petty; I don't even think about it; I don't worry about it. I say we just focus on that which we want to do, which is good for the school. I'm able to leave, to sleep at night.

JA: You're able to bracket all of that?

SM: Yes. I don't even think about it, honestly; I don't even know if there are fights; I don't even care, not because I want to do that but for my health. I can't afford to be fighting, honestly. I think I'm just at work here, just like they are. If anybody wants to fight me, it should be my wife at home or something!

JA: Being in your position, you have to make difficult ethical decisions all the time. Sometimes you're going to disappoint people; you're going to upset people, even if you're trying to be helpful and supportive.

SM: Yes, and that would kill me; I don't want that. I've discovered that I'm more critical of myself than other people are. I don't want to be in that state. For example, if I do something that I feel may have hurt this person, it takes time for me to really heal. The pain is very much with me, so I try to avoid it by not engaging in that. Ultimately, I have done this so often that it has become part of my nature; I don't even think about it sometimes. It's possible that I've disappointed some people, but honestly it's unintentional. If I would be aware of that, it would really kill me if I'm not able to correct it; that's how I think. I have trained myself to look at those things that are positive about people. There are always two sides of a story.

There's a saying. I can't remember where I got that: Everybody is an enemy until they prove themselves otherwise. I've tried to turn that around, that everybody is a good person until they prove themselves differently; that is how I tend to look at things. There's that goodness we can still find if we look close enough. If we are patient enough to look very closely, we definitely are going to see something very good.

JA: In Mandela's autobiography [*Long Walk to Freedom*] he talks about how he befriended his prison guard on Robben Island. He had this deep-seated belief that there was always some good part of a human being, despite how the external reality might be quite different.

SM: It's true. This, I think, is what makes me to survive because I'm able to see that. If you're able to see that, the other person can see that you're seeing it, and it becomes easier to relate and interact; I struggle with it. It is also informed by my own understanding of social class, stuff like that, for example, homeless people who would be easy to dismiss. I've discovered that if I have the time to talk and engage, there is always that beauty, that human thing, that wonderful thing about them, irrespective of where they are. It's a question of time and patience. If you give anybody that opportunity, it's really that goodness that will always come out: everybody, even the right wingers, and so on. I just gave you the example of this guy who was so angry with me when I started here, and I couldn't understand what was really wrong.

JA: That's a good segue into the next question. What are the greatest personal and institutional challenges for you in practicing leadership for social justice at the UFS?

SM: I'm really not able to think of many challenges because almost everything that I try to put together and put my mind to, it happens: I haven't had serious challenges. Maybe I'm insulated where I am; I don't know. I make my own decisions, and the only person I have to convince is Dennis [Professor Dennis Frances, former dean of the Faculty of Education], who incidentally agrees with me because he actually can see some of those things; honestly, I don't know. Maybe it could be, at my own personal level, to remember all the codes for the motion detectors because some of them don't make sense!

There's just a minor incident, not really a challenge. I thought this person understood that we can produce quality and we are black. Recently, I was just having a light moment talking about faculty who have generated so much money, a stream of income, and how I would really like to be friends with them; it's always good to have rich friends! This person said, "You too have money. And I said, "Yes I do but not as much as those people have generated." Then this person said, "I wish I was black too." It really took me aback because I had expected that this person would understand that to win funding at whatever level, it's not about being black. I think the justification was that I'm also good, but I'm the wrong race. If that was what was implied, then it becomes a challenge. I thought this person understood what it takes because to produce a proposal, you really have to spend time and focus on that, which maybe the person didn't have. It's just one of those minor things – to strike a balance around race.

Today, I went for this micro teaching. In micro teaching we have finishing students, fourth-year student teachers. They have to do their presentation on particular skills. Sometimes they practice with the introduction, others with the use of media, or something like that. This year one young black person joined our staff. In the teaching class he is the only black person in there with two white people. In the beginning of the year, there is all this confusion.

Someone wrote me an e-mail to say that this black guy did not attend class: How am I handling the situation? Then I went out to find out and discovered that actually it was one of these white people. I didn't write back, so I had an opportunity to talk with the person. I met with the person and asked, "By the way, why did you think it was the black teacher?" The person apologized immediately and even wrote an e-mail to apologize. I wrote back to say that really it doesn't matter, that the problem has been solved. The same person came to the micro teaching class today. When the person opened the door, I was looking in that direction. The person peeked in, then waved, and went away. I suspect that the person wanted to make sure that I was there, which I think shows a lack of trust, if the person was going to check whether I was there. The person assumes that I'm so much interested in research, for example, that I regard teaching as not important, whereas I really think the two are equally important.

As head of school I have to be exemplary – do those kinds of things that teachers in a university generally like to do. What I'm trying to say is the question of race is still an issue for me to the extent that I feel between

40 *M.G. Sechaba Mahlomaholo*

that negative stereotyping, racism, and whatever, and us; it's only Dennis. I think if it [the deanship of the Faculty of Education] were one of them [was held by an Afrikaner], we would not even be where we are; that is constantly on my mind. Some of these incidents remind me. Maybe I'm misinterpreting things, possibly, but things happen so frequently, you really are never sure. It's still the same thing that you have in Potchefstroom. It's just that here it's under the carpet: People have to produce evidence that we're not performing. If we were elsewhere they would even be dismissed without being given the opportunity.

JA: So they're constantly looking for evidence to undermine your leadership?

SM: I am consciously aware that I'm under surveillance at all times and for the wrong reasons. It's something that I am personally aware of, which I think would be a challenge, but I'm not thinking about it a lot. I'm in a context where nobody mentions that. In fact, I think my colleagues are very happy because one thing about the people that I'm working with, they're so open. If there is something you're not doing right, they will tell you!

I really had serious occasions where, if anything, they should have said something. I don't know what they could have said from the other side – maybe we are doing this – but I think it's more competition and fear because they've been here all along, and all of sudden, in two years, things have become so different. I'm really being honest here, that many of them [white colleagues], they really look very ordinary, and where even color doesn't matter because we are being evaluated by systems outside our control. I think it's more of that.

They've never generated any funding, all the time finding out how much the university can give them. They've never supervised any students; they're always blaming students and saying how lazy they are. Our system has been different, honestly, and we have seen positive outcomes. Last year we had five people graduate with a PhD in two years, in an average of two years, which they haven't seen before. I think if they even had two or so, it would really be a big issue. It would be in the media!

JA: You're actually judged on merit and outputs now rather than your complexion, so it's a whole different ball game.

SM: I've always wished for that challenge – where we would be evaluated on what is it that we can do, not who we are. Unfortunately, the world is organized around those things [performance outcomes metrics]. We're better able to do certain things. All the time we are told about research output; we have to talk about that all the time, talk about postgraduate throughputs [graduation rates]. We have to reorganize our lives around that, not only as individuals but as institutions.

For example, this NRF [National Research Foundation, an independent government agency that promotes and supports research and rates the scholarship of academics in South Africa] rating thing, I've never done it. I didn't think it was important until I realized that if I do it, the institution

The question of fairness 41

looks good, so then I had to go through that process. I don't believe in competition as something that drives life, but if given no alternative, I'm not afraid; I can and do engage. This is where some people sometimes misunderstand what I describe as invitational leadership as being afraid. Honestly, I'm not; it's a choice that I'm making. If it comes to push where I have no other choice, I have to resort to the same strategies as conventional people. I am capable of that, but I try not to do that. I resort to that as a last measure before I die! It's uncomfortable.

JA: Did some white colleagues think you had an agenda, a racial agenda, when you arrived?

SM: Yes, that and some other things. When they realized there was nothing, even the initial resistance just melted away. Because it had to be based on substance, and then we were talking about outcomes; we were talking about productivity, which everybody had to abide by. When you go out there [in the hallway next to his office], we've put up our articles, which is a way of really showing off to the other schools but at the same time to encourage everybody.

I can tell you that I had been trying to apply for a position at this university for over five years, and I never even got an acknowledgement of receipt of my application. Even when I got here, people were very suspicious that maybe there was something that we intended doing. Even when I got here, I got the same kind of suspicion. But after some time, people opened up to realize there was nothing really.

I came here in 2011, but I've been in Bloemfontein before, so this was like coming for the second time. I know many of these guys [other black faculty members], and we have been elsewhere where we really fought very hard and won in many instances. They still know what we can do. They are waiting for me, for us and Milton [Dr. Molebatsi Nkoane], to do certain things, and nothing is happening. I think this was where the fear came from because we came from Vista, the southern campus [Vista University, a historically black institution, became the southern campus of the UFS in 2004], and we really would engage them seriously.

It's about output, and really there's nothing else; it's all that we have to do. That's why we are all here. It's not about who's doing what; it doesn't matter. Archbishop [Desmond] Tutu was making an example that if someone would rescue you out of a boat that was destined to capsize, would you ask that person whether he was a communist or what before he does that? It really didn't matter. What was important was whether the job is done. If he saved you, and he was a communist, fine, he'll go to hell!

JA: While you're willing to fight for fairness and justice, you do not necessarily take a confrontational approach.

SM: Maybe if a person would call me a *kaffir* [a racial epithet], I would have no option there; I would have to respond immediately. There were such incidents [at the Potchefstroom campus of North West University], and I reacted in a very confrontational manner. On the basis of that I've been able to move on because that would be an isolated incident, honestly. I really haven't experienced a serious situation. On the whole, my view that people are good is reinforced all the time, and I regard those as outliers. You'd have bad black people anyway, who mug you sometimes or do some bad things. On the basis of that I am not able to generalize. Those bad incidents are far apart, and I've found a way of avoiding them. I will confront them if they are really in my face all the time. But if they're not, I am able to look at other important things.

Somebody told me that you are better able to see and hear some things if you're blind, in a way, when people least suspect that you'll fight or do anything. You are able to interact and to relate, and there's no problem, unlike if you'd be confrontational. Actually, in our language they tell a story of how you would get a calf, a young cow, into a *kraal* [a pen] without having to beat it up. The strategy is you pull it by the tail, and it will want to spite you and move into the *kraal* because it is thinking it does not want to; I think that's one way. They really get immobilized. They don't know what to do because they're gearing themselves up for something. You make it very unnecessary, and then really, the problem is how to respond next. I try to do the easy thing because the alternative is hectic, and it takes a heavy toll emotionally and otherwise.

JA: I know Dennis [Dennis Francis, former dean of the Faculty of Education] recruited people, like yourself and Milton [Dr. Molebatsi Nkoane], who previously knew each other and worked together at other universities. In that way, some of the black networks that existed outside of the UFS were brought into the Faculty of Education. Has that been significant in terms of support for your leadership?

SM: Really, in very many ways. Our SULE [Sustainable Learning Environments and Social Justice] colloquium is one example. Those people who are there, we've been with them for a long time and have been doing many things. We've been going to the institutions. We've been doing all kinds of things with our international friends and many other people. We're keeping that network, international and locally. They [white colleagues opposed to blacks in positions of leadership] wouldn't dare want to make any problem because they are aware that there are many people that we relate with. Even if they would come up with a bad story, it would really take a lot to convince them that this person has really done this bad thing, deliberately became racist or something. I think the network is cushioning us against that activity. Even before people want to do certain things, they are aware that it's not just me; there are many people. That also helps to validate us in a way. It's not like I'm this lone wolf doing this mad thing.

JA: There's a lot of talk about transformation at the UFS. It means different things to different people and has been politicized, especially in the context of universities. What does transformation mean to you? How is it related to your leadership?

SM: I'm always looking at our Faculty of Education, what it looked like. It was 99.9% white, and mainly white males, mainly Afrikaans all the time. But now it has become a different place. People talk about quality to say that when black people come on board, that quality goes down: It hasn't happened. Actually, the opposite has. That's what I understand by transformation: creating opportunities for everybody that contribute to quality. I've read also in the literature that in some of the schools, they're saying that [quality goes down] in high-performing white schools, especially white schools if you get black kids there. Some parents would even take their kids away, you see, because that would compromise quality. But the literature says that if you introduce diversity, then things tend to get better. Even if you introduce slow children into a group of high-performing kids, the slow ones are going to pull the bright ones. Actually, the bright ones will get even brighter because now they have the opportunity of learning from their perspective and also from the perspective of the slower ones.

Because this institution was exclusively Afrikaans, just like Potchefstroom, I'm feeling there's a great potential if these people can realize that we belong to the same team and not to want to do us down; because if they do, it is not in their own interest as well. But if they would collaborate, we would be even better, like UCT [University of Cape Town] or some of the respected universities. This is my understanding of transformation, that you create space.

I think you've also seen from the journal pieces [research presented at the SULE colloquium was published in special issues of two journals] that many of the people who publish, this is their first time publishing. Because if you concentrate on high-publishing people only, I think you reach a ceiling. There are about, let's say, 50 of us. If each one has one article, then we have a big capacity, unlike if you had four people publishing 10 articles each; it's almost impossible. For me, transformation means broadening participation and access and making it possible for everybody to publish. Then everybody wins; nobody is strained. Unlike in the past, there was just one professor who was publishing. If that person would get ill or something, then it would be a big problem!

Making it possible for everyone to succeed, you can't do that alone. Nobody can do that. If we understand the bigger picture, that it's about our institution, then it should work well. In the end, we're making it possible for everybody to do their best. But some people come from a culture that says: I'm better than so and so; I got a few articles, and my neighbor got nothing. But what's the point? But if all of us do a little bit of everything, then all of us move nicely together.

JA: Are there other important aspects of leadership that we haven't talked about?
SM: Leadership: it's a space. Many people come in and go off. It's true that you interview me as a person, but I represent so many people's aspirations and efforts. I'm a climaxing of those experiences, if I can put it that way. When

you interact with me, you interact with my parents, who contributed a bit of what they did to who I am; you interact with other people also, my students, although I was their leader, or supervisor, or teacher. Then in the process I have relied so much, borrowed and learned so many things from them.

Yes, it's true, you look at me now, but I think in all fairness, it's not just me that you're interacting with. You're interacting with the whole history of experiences of people. I only realized how limited most probably I could be, or I am, without all those experiences. I may have been responding to you as one individual, but the point I want to make is that you have that mass of people; this is what really sustains, keeps sustaining us. I'm not able to say me, this is I, but I think there have been all these bits and pieces of contributions from all kinds of people. Those that have been successful from my perspective have been those that have been operating in the manner in which I'm trying to define and position myself, taking a cue from what they did and what they're doing.

I think in the whole narrative, the whole story, what makes it interesting for you is because you can recognize yourself in what I'm saying; this is what makes it interesting for you. I mean, no other person has taken that interest. Maybe I should not say no other. Other people who don't think like you have not contributed in the same manner towards creating. They would not find it interesting to listen to that; they can't see it. But it becomes interesting for you because it is how you look at things. You can actually see, in what I'm saying, you can actually see yourself. I think this is what makes it so interesting for you and for me as well.

JA: Our experiences are quite different, but I can certainly see myself in how you understand things in some ways. I can only begin to imagine what kind of struggles you had to deal with to get to where you are today. Growing up in townships under apartheid, dealing with all that, and somehow you managed to not let that crush you, and to remain positive, not only positive but genuinely believing in the goodness of individuals. Somehow protecting yourself not only physically, but psychologically as well, and emotionally, from the kind of damage that could have been inflicted on you.

SM: Well, I think you hear from my story that I may have wanted to do that. But if it were not for the whole environment that created me, and later on other people, I don't think it could have been possible. Honestly, that's why I'm so eternally grateful for the many people that I'd had. If the story was about me, my own personal story, then from what my father did took over indirectly to create the same whole environment.

JA: I want to switch gears here and talk more about your intellectual development and how your thinking evolved over time, what sort of theories and discourses influenced your thinking. One topic that may be relevant is the question of the liberation struggle. Does your experience of the liberation struggle inform your understanding and practice of leadership for social justice?

The question of fairness 45

SM: Yes, definitely it does. In terms of my political orientation, I have been in what you call the Black Consciousness Movement, not in the ANC. This has been a driving force in my life. To some extent I consider myself to be privileged because my parents, relatively, were enlightened. They were aware that giving a good education is important, like many of our black parents were. But they really made an effort to take us to school. My father has passed on. Materially he hasn't left me anything. But what he gave me in terms of education really managed to sustain me to this day. There was even this destabilization in my life. What protected me was that education that he gave me. Otherwise, I would be out in the wilderness, and really I would not know what to do. One thing that really insulated me was that which he gave me, which is far better than if he had given me a farm or something material, which maybe it would have been gone now, maybe sold, or I would have gambled it off or something! I consider that very important.

It has always been my wish that one could plow back and really do something that would make it possible for other people who were less fortunate than I was to really have access to some of the things, to some extent, I could have access to. This is what has really been at the back of my mind, an awareness of how privileged I was compared to the majority of other black people my age in many respects. Secondly, I was consciously aware of the many sacrifices that many people had made to create a space and a platform for me in particular to pursue the kind of things I wanted to pursue. That has really been a powerful motivator.

For me, I didn't have to do the extremes. I went to the U.S. [to obtain a master's degree at Harvard University], for example, in the 80s, and I met these exiles with no hope of ever coming back to the country. But for me, I would be coming back; I just had to finish my studies. Those were powerful experiences. I just have to do what I can do well, and it's not even a sacrifice I can write home about because basically it's nothing. I'm actually being paid to read, to write, to supervise, to teach, whereas some of these guys had no sources of income whatever, but they still did that. How shall I put that? I realized how much I owed so many people.

JA: That's a good segue into my next question. You attended the University of the North as an undergraduate, where you got your UED in education, far from where your family was living. The campus is near Polokwane in Limpopo province. As I understand it, the University of the North was a major center of student protest in the 60s, 70s, and 80s. I think you were there around 1977, when the entire student body was expelled. How did that affect your thinking?

SM: Honestly, in the same vein, the same way of thinking, it was a minor sacrifice to make, although it was costly at the same time. I think we went to the university about three or four times; sometimes on the way we'd hear on the radio that the university was open. We were traveling these thousands of kilometers by train, which in one direction would generally take you two

46   *M.G. Sechaba Mahlomaholo*

to three days to complete, with very little resources because we depended 100% on the parents and so on; it was costly in that sense. But at the same time there was a sense that it was for a good reason. Also, compared to what other people had to sacrifice, that was nothing.

There was hope. All of us, we knew what the alternative was, that if we didn't do what we did, the alternative was too ghastly to contemplate. We felt bad; we felt that we were losing, but at the same time I think like these guys in Marikana [a platinum mine near Johannesburg where 36 striking miners were killed by police in 2013]. They stayed for six months at home without pay; it's a major sacrifice. But many of them are very happy with what they have achieved because it's really addressing the social transformations in the country. That you'd have a mining company that has been taking minerals out of the country for 150 years and they had nothing to show. Even this 1000 rand [approximately 68 U.S. dollars] extra that they're asking, it really doesn't mean much. Even the sacrifice they've gone through is nothing compared to the conscientization [an English translation of the Portuguese term *conscientiçazão*, which in the context of BCM (the Black Consciousness Movement), refers to the process of spreading political awareness] that they have managed to achieve.

It was the same kind of feeling then, if one would understand the spirit of the times: it was 1976. It affected us directly because it meant that we were now going to be taught subjects in Afrikaans in 1976, and we saw that if we really did not stand up, even for others, we were like in a role now to say that we just have to continue because the possibility of succeeding was very great. We lost a year, but at another level it really didn't matter because we knew it was a better investment for the future.

JA: At the University of the North, the South African Students' Organization (SASO) was a leading Black Consciousness group. In fact, the University of the North was their best-organized campus in the country. This was beginning in the early 1970s when you were still in high school. Were you influenced by the Black Consciousness Movement, or by Black Consciousness discourse, as a high school student? When did your own process of conscientization begin?

SM: In fact, there was no way that you could have become otherwise. The times were such; you had to because the oppression, you felt it directly – access to many things. This was the period of the Bantustans [the 'independent' homelands created for blacks under apartheid], where even movement was restricted. We were forced to stay in QwaQwa [one of the 10 homelands]; that was the area that we would be confined to.

I stayed in Ladybrand, which is far from QwaQwa; there were no high schools there. If I wanted to go to [high] school, I had to go there [to QwaQwa]. You start asking yourself a number of questions: Why was I not able to go to school at home? Why was I here? Even better, competent peers could not proceed just because the high schools were not where they were. There were contradictions, materially, that made you aware of what it means to be a black person.

The question of fairness 47

With many of the uprisings at the University of the North, then the students there were expelled. I think that created, like a seed; they went all over. Some of them came to teach us in those schools. There was one person in particular I still remember. His name was Botho; that is his real name, meaning black. This guy had not completed his degree. He taught us everything. In the schools that we were at, we didn't even have teachers. This guy went out of his way to teach us history, to teach us mathematics, to teach us physical science at Grade 12. The manner in which he taught us, it was inspiring to us, making us realize the great possibilities that would be there for us. He was not a full-fledged teacher; this was a university student, a dropout student. Those were some of the inspirations. He was not alone; there were a few others that got us interested and excited and inspired.

When I went to University of the North, the Black Consciousness Movement, the SASO organization, was not there anymore; it was crushed. They clamped down; there were all kinds of things happening since 1976. When I went to the university in 1976, those political formations were not there. But in their place there were new ones that were created because much of the leadership was in prison. I participated in the new ones, but cautiously. I was not vocal; I participated and went to the meetings. I did everything, protested, stayed out, whatever, but I was not in the leadership then. When we completed university, then we could not run away from that; we had to take leadership roles. I must say I chose the easier, the softer option.

I was teaching. What I did was to infuse that which I was teaching into the curriculum. I found an opportunity to really conscientize the students. Because it was easy to say you just have to be proud of ourselves, and work hard, and protect our interests, and love our fellow human beings. Those were easy things to say and teach and to inspire that pride in the students in everything that we did. For me, that was an easy thing to do, an easy option, the softer option compared to having to go into exile or joining the military wing of the ANC: That I didn't do.

JA: I know the Black Consciousness Movement was strongly influenced by black theology. Given the importance of Christianity for you in your thinking and what you do, did black theology, through the Black Consciousness Movement, influence you?

SM: Yes, to a very large extent in many ways. We called it liberation theology that one read extensively. I could find a lot of compatibility between what the liberation struggle was about and the theological teachings in Christianity in particular and from the works of many South African scholars: Allan Boesak and many others. The South African Council of Churches (SACC) was at the forefront of the liberation struggle during that time. Especially when I started working, there would be very serious strikes, protestations, where the police would be very brutal, and the people who provided bail for the students, and for us and for whatever, was the SACC. We had that direct contact with them. They would be there to get lawyers and to go in and assist students to be released from prisons and so on. The influence was very powerful.

48 *M.G. Sechaba Mahlomaholo*

My exposure to people like Farrakhan [Minister Luis Farrakhan, the leader of the Nation of Islam], and Malcolm X [a leading proponent of black nationalism], and a few other American black people's consciousness movements. There was really a lot of reading that influenced my thinking around that, which assisted me to theorize and to understand better the kind of things we were doing, the kind of oppression that we are faced with. The theories that we came up with were very incisive. But I realized at the same time that this was not palatable, even currently. Because we were comparing all the time Steve Biko and Nelson Mandela, and we could understand why one was killed and the other one was spared. Because one is just about reformation, it's not about a radical transformation of society, as Steve Biko preached it. That kind of thing is still at the back of my mind, honestly, I must say, the great respect that we had for Steve Biko and the kind of things that he was preaching.

JA: Since Christianity is so central to your identity, were you ever a member of the University Christian movement? Were you part of that?

SM: Yes, I was. I've never preached. I'm not able to even make a loud prayer. In church they say come and pray, but I've never done that. I've been in those movements. I've assisted in many ways but not being in a leadership position; I've always followed. To some extent I feel religion and faith, maybe it's a very personal thing. I understand also that you need social structures, social organization, to be able to pursue that. I've never really felt like I want to influence it in the manner I'm trying to; I feel comfortable just following. I've always been in Christian organizations but not to the extent that I've been in the academic setting. I've just followed, and I'm comfortable with that.

The climaxing of my reading ultimately pushes me to the realization that this Christian thing perhaps is the right thing for me to believe in. I've been reading a lot on discourses, analyses of discourses, ideologies, the power of words, and so on, and that led me to understanding more that in the beginning was the word. I understand how identities are created in conversations and so on. I'm beginning to understand what that biblical text actually says. In the beginning was the word, and we are created through the word. Maybe I'm reading too much into it. That has suffused my reading and my understanding. I really find I can argue, but there comes a position which I cannot argue beyond. For me, to try and make sense, I have to insert a quote. I find that very comforting.

JA: I want to talk about some of the ideas in your writings and how they relate to your thinking. In two of your pieces you use [Antonio] Gramsci's notion of organic intellectuals to illustrate what you believe should be the role of researchers in terms of conscientizing communities, of having this organic relationship to the community, this passionate kind of connection to the people that you're working with. Is your understanding of Gramsci's notion of organic intellectuals informed by your understanding of the Black Consciousness Movement? You use the word conscientizing in your

The question of fairness 49

writings, which comes right out of Paulo Freire and the Black Consciousness Movement.

SM: Definitely, it does come out of that. This whole Black Conscious theory influenced everything in my life. I'm not able to theorize, to understand outside of that. When you look at Gramsci from my perspective, he is trying to describe the situation that I'm experiencing, that I'm going through, which I tried to refer to earlier, my upbringing and actually feeling privileged; all the time I really felt that way. I felt I really have to do something in order to fully exploit that position in which I was. There's a piece I wrote with a woman from Venda [the University of Venda], which we presented in Prague or somewhere, where we're talking about that notion of Gramsci to say we see our role, our position as black academics, as that space of contradiction, where we're coming into that space with these resources, with these privileges of a bourgeois academic institution and lifestyle that we have acquired. But at the same time, reminding us consistently that we have to do a lot in order to bring as many of our people maybe to the same space, use the resources of the university to bring up the communities out of this abject poverty and whatever problems they may be experiencing. That has been powerful.

At the same time, it was kind of a reflection on our part to see that theory of us as an opportunity to reflect on who we really are. We have become different people. The pains that the majority of the black people are experiencing, none of us experienced that. One has to approach that with great caution and great understanding. For example, I no longer even stay in the township. I'm going to church in Ladybrand, my home, which is one and a half hours from here. While I did it initially because I felt my father was in that church, it's nice to be with those people. But at the same time I realize that maybe there's this awareness, that maybe I've become removed from the experiences, and the one way to really come into touch with who I really am is going back there. At the same time, I'm aware of how condescending that could be, like a tourist going into an informal settlement, the arrogance of saying I'm different, that I'm better maybe.

I've been trying to do that but at the same time very critical of that. Maybe I have to do it more respectfully because it really is not about that. Honestly, it's about me trying to come in touch with myself, that this is who I should be. This is where I come from; this is me. I've been removed, or I've moved out so that I still have to maintain the relationship. Sometimes if you're that far and removed materially and otherwise in space and time, then it can damage you because you no longer experience the feelings that used to inspire you, that used to be there for you to understand who you really are.

I think this is what happens to many of the black middle-class people like me. Sometimes it influences even their thinking and the manner in which they do things. It pushes them into the direction of arrogance and false superiority complexes that do not assist. I've met many such people who really feel that the world is made for them and that people owe them some things and who do not have the sensitivity.

50 M.G. Sechaba Mahlomaholo

I listen carefully to how you're talking about these ladies who are working in our settings [the black women who clean the campus residences], the respectful manner in which you refer to them. There's a possibility that because of one's material whatever, you'd use words like *maid, nannies,* or things like that, saying they are less of humans. I see this in some of my kids because I've been able to take them to some of these middle-class schools. They come back with attitudes that I really find very strange. All the time I have to remind them – this is their mother's work – because I know what it means. For them, it's just not even a helper; it's just a maid. It's a consciousness that I really try to keep. That notion of the organic intellectual, I think this is what keeps us sane all the time. Yes, you may have achieved that, but that's not really where you should be. You consistently have to remind yourself that you truly become who you are if you keep in touch with those experiences that are more authentic and genuine, if I can use such concepts.

Because then you will know where to go. Otherwise you become someone without a compass; you don't even know why you do certain things. That grounding for me has been helpful. Even sometimes where I would forget, that thing still reminds me: Maybe you don't even deserve to be where you are. It's because of other people's hard work and sacrifices, which you have to be respectful of. Having realized how many of the good students that we were in class with, many of them, they're nowhere now; others have died. When you look at them, you realize life has not been good to them, and you realize how fortunate you have been. It's not just you working out, but there have been those insulating experiences that made you at least to succeed. You still ask yourself, again, the religious thing: Why me? What made the difference? I could easily have been in that category. Those realizations, I think, keep one focused to realize how privileged you are. There should have been a reason, obviously. Maybe you would really have to do certain things in order to recognize the support.

I talked about my father a lot, but I also realized the inputs of many people, many people that came along to really make the dream to be real and to be realized; some of them don't even have anything. Ultimately, when you get there you have to recognize that it's not just that it's out of your own effort, if your role is to create opportunities for other people in the same manner that other people did that for you. Some of those people did that for you, not even knowing who you are. There's that bigger mission, I think, that you get reminded of because of the notion of the organic intellectual, where you have to straddle two worlds carefully, be able to achieve certain things but still remember who you are all the time.

JA: You begin your inaugural lecture at North West University by retelling the story of the rupturing and dismemberment, both metaphorically and literally, of African identity through the experience of an enslaved African woman named Saartjie Baartman, who was taken to London and Paris and put on public display. You use her example to illustrate the fracturing of African identity into what you call bits and pieces. How is this sense of fracturing understood and addressed in your practice of leadership? How does it inform you thinking?

SM: I read these post-structuralist stories around the construction of identity and that kind of thing. There is a concept, I think it is a French phrase, *corps morcelé*, referring to how children are immediately at birth, maybe until the age of six – he [the French psychoanalyst and philosopher Jacques Lacan] doesn't put ages there – when the existential moment occurs, when children are beginning to stand outside of themselves and realize that, after all, they are this one indivisible being. Before then, it's in a state of bits and pieces, incoherent, where they do not even have control over their fingers and many of their motor activities. My understanding therefore, is that it serves as a metaphor for what apartheid and colonialism had done to Africa, to Africans, to black people in general.

Whatever sense of being we may have had before, this has been broken down, put asunder, broken into bits and pieces. Our role, in whatever position we are, is to try and bring that together, maybe not only as black or African but maybe as South Africans. We really need to come together and have a sense of cohesion, a sense of identity, a sense of a commonality of peoples. Because it's only in that sense, operated at and beyond the existential moment, where we're able to self-reflect, to see ourselves as this undividable unity. It's about pride, about inspiring hope, about despair and hope, about making it possible for us to imagine a better world beyond that which we may be experiencing currently. It's a way of bringing about a sense of people's being. I think in terms of leadership, that is also what is motivating me.

One of the objections [from a white colleague in the Faculty of Education] was that we were getting into our team students who do not qualify. My argument has been that we have not tapped into the abilities of these people. If we rely on their previous performances, none of those would be able to be prognostic enough, accurately, to say who these people could be. I make it possible for some of those students to come in who were destined for what I call the social dustbins, thrown away. They have grown into becoming very strong and ultimately have become leaders in their own right. I've seen that happening many times. That says to me, given the appropriate support, they can achieve beyond anybody's wildest expectations. It's just a question of validation, supporting and creating the material conditions for that to happen.

Significance and implications

What is most striking about Professor Mahlomaholo's remarks is not only his generosity of spirit, but the deeply-felt empathy and compassion he has for poor and oppressed people, for those who were excluded and marginalized, and his ethical commitment to provide them with opportunities to cultivate their capacities, to remove themselves from the 'social dustbins' to which they have been relegated.

His approach to leadership is to give people an opportunity to reveal to themselves, and to others, what they are capable of achieving, and is marked by a deep trust and abiding faith in the essential goodness of human beings. Professor Mahlomaholo's acute sensitivity to the pain of others is reflected in the guiding principle of his leadership: Do unto others as you would like them to do unto you. For him, leadership is not about ego fulfillment, self-aggrandizement, or the exercise of power, but instead requires a sense of humility and a recognition that we all stand on the shoulders of others who made our achievements possible. In his view, educational leaders should have affective connections to the people and communities they serve, and help them "imagine a future which is different and full of possibilities" (Mahlomaholo & Netshandama, 2010, p. 9).

References

Mahlomaholo, M.G. (August 21, 2009). Inaugural lecture. *Remembering the organic intellectual in the mirror*. Potchefstroom: North West University.

Mahlomaholo, M.G. & Netshandama, V. (2010). *Sustainable empowering learning environments: Conversations with Gramsci's organic intellectual*. Retrieved from http://www.inter-disciplinary.net/wp-content/uploads/2010/04/Mahlomaholo-paper.pdf

4 Something much bigger
Doing what is good and what is right

B.R. Rudi Buys

Reverend B.R. Rudi Buys was the dean of Student Affairs at the UFS from 2010 to 2014, where he led efforts to integrate previously all-white residence halls and change cultural traditions to be more inclusive and respectful. An ordained minister in the Dutch Reformed Church, his notion of leadership is strongly influenced and informed by his spiritual beliefs and ethical commitments. Like his father, who was also a minister in the Church, Reverend Buys is part of a liberal religious tradition inspired by the life and work of Reverend Beyers Naudé, a courageous and outspoken critic of apartheid. In fact, Reverend Buys was ordained into the ministry with the same gown that was once worn by him. Reverend Buys was born in Clocolan in the eastern Free State of South Africa, but grew up in northern and southern Namibia.

Reverend Buys earned undergraduate degrees in practical theology and political science and a master's degree in theology and political science from Stellenbosch University and is a PhD candidate in higher education at the UFS. He served as the Western Cape Youth commissioner and spokesperson for the Western Cape Education Ministry and was a cofounder and chief executive officer of the iGubu Leadership Agency, which assists universities in South Africa with racial conflict resolution, reconciliation, and change programming. Most recently, Reverend Buys was a visiting graduate scholar at the University of Southern California, Los Angeles, Graduate School of Education & Information Studies.

In 2008 the iGubu Leadership Agency was brought in by the acting rector to address issues of racial conflict on the campus in the wake of the Reitz incident [in which four white students humiliated five black employees of the UFS]. In response, the agency developed the Residences Diversity Project (RDP), which was implemented over a two-year period. In January 2010, Reverend Buys, who as CEO of the iGubu Leadership Agency was deeply involved in developing and implementing the RDP, was appointed dean of Student Affairs.

As dean of Student Affairs, Reverend Buys was charged with racially integrating and transforming the culture of the residence halls, which was a daunting task given that the UFS was a historically Afrikaner institution for a century before the new democratic dispensation in 1994. Many Afrikaner students, their families, and their allies in the Afrikaner community and media viewed these changes as

54   B.R. *Rudi Buys*

an existential threat and an attack on their culture, traditions, and racial privilege, and fiercely opposed the efforts of Reverend Buys.

While he faced many challenges in seeking to successfully implement a diversity project, one incident that received a significant amount of attention, especially from the Afrikaans media, involved the JBM Hertzog residence hall [named after a former prime minister of South Africa who supported racial policies that increased the segregation and disenfranchisement of blacks]. The JBM residence hall, similar to other men's residences on the Bloemfontein campus, maintained several inhumane and degrading cultural traditions, including one that involved showering first-year women. The men would organize a social with a women's residence. After the women arrived at the residence, the men would shout out the names of women and take them to the showers and shower them. However, the women were given a choice: They could shower with cold water with their clothes on or shower with hot water but without their clothes.

Reverend Buys was determined the end this and other humiliating practices. However, after three years of fruitless discussions with student leaders at JBM, during which time Reverend Buys sought to involve them in designing new traditions to replace this offensive practice, he announced at a meeting of the residents that the practice, known as *tikkie*, would no longer be allowed and explained the reasoning behind the decision. Some students at the meeting voiced their strong opposition to the new policy, sometimes in angry and disrespectful ways, and accused Reverend Buys of being authoritarian and imposing his views on them.

Without his knowledge, a student at the meeting secretly recorded the discussion, which was subsequently posted on the Internet and shared with the Afrikaans media. Some students, mostly Afrikaner, organized noisy protests outside the building that houses the Office of Student Affairs and presented Reverend Buys with a petition demanding that he rescind the new policy. At the same time, Reverend Buys was being vilified in the local and national Afrikaans media, which accused him, in effect, of being a race traitor for insisting that this degrading practice come to an end and that public spaces in the residence halls reflect the diverse histories, identities, and cultural practices of all students at the UFS.

The JBM incident is just one example of the racial minefield that individuals who practice leadership for transformation and social justice at the UFS must navigate every day in attempting to implement policies that seek to dismantle racialized and gendered structures of power and privilege, and the culture of white supremacy, at historically Afrikaner universities.

In a public lecture at the UFS (Buys, October 27, 2014), in front of an audience comprised mostly of students, Reverend Buys reflected on why the cultural change project at JBM generated so much anger and resistance. After critically analyzing his approach to resolving the impasse, Reverend Buys concluded that he and other university administrators had set themselves up for failure by imagining that their relations with students had somehow changed and that they were no longer based on a hierarchy of power because students were engaged in a values-based discussion of the transformation process. The problem, he found, was that administrators and students were still acting on the basis of a structural notion of power and change in which each side seeks to become the dominant player in setting the rules. By making a decision to end the shower tradition over the vehement protests of many students, he had simply replaced one hierarchy with another, namely, that of power with one of values.

To remedy this situation, Reverend Buys suggested that management shift from a focus on the structural relations of power to the relations among people in their emotional interactions and to lead with trust and faith in the possibility of moving beyond the past. Rather than impose a hierarchy of values on students, the aim of the administration, he argued, should be to cultivate a community of shared aspirations *driven* by values rather than merely *based on* values. This involves assisting students in deconstructing 'how we live together' and engaging them in a process of creating new aspirations driven by values. This is a challenging approach for educational leaders because it requires a leap of faith based on a relationship of trust, a firm belief that students will ultimately do 'what is good and right and just.' It also requires that leaders have sufficient patience to allow the process to unfold.

Reverend Buys began our conversation by discussing what leadership for social justice means to him in the context of contemporary South Africa.

RB: The first thought that jumped to mind, the key word, is to be caring, to really want to change. To give it a bit more of a sense, I think to lead for social justice in our country, in our context, means to integrate a number of things in your own thinking and being – making sense of the world first or trying to shift and change the world to a better world, basically. For me, social justice is, of course, to deal with these three and our best aspirations for the future. And that is based on the fact that you really care for people, care for all people – not some of the people but all of the people. They care about fairness and freedom and equality and all these things.

My point being is that it's first a life to be lived before a job to be achieved or a cause to be realized. Leadership for social justice isn't something out there but something in here before you can actually achieve it out there. For me, social justice first brings the question of who you are, and what you think about yourself, and your place in the world, and your place among people, then, of course, in conjunction with your reflection on the history of our country and how that relates to our future. And what your dreams should be: the best ideas that we've had in our country, the best ideas of freedom for everyone, in all respects. Because these things were missing in our country, fairness and equality and what people would be.

JA: So for you, social justice is a way of life rather than an abstract concept.
RB: It's a way of being. For me, a central conversation or discussion on issues of social justice is around ethics and not about ethical protocols or ethical frameworks or codes of ethical conduct but your own fundamental principled sense, or awareness and self-awareness, of ethical conduct, of principled conduct, value-driven engagement with yourself. But I might be a bit

56   *B.R. Rudi Buys*

idealistic in terms of that. But for me, practice is a core question. How do you claim to want to build a world of social justice in view of a history of where it's absent? When in your own heart, in your own mind, in your own life, in your own family, in your own sort of self-conversation, you don't attempt to have that conversation? Then you're not leading for social justice.

JA: How does this understanding inform your conception and practice of leadership?

RB: For me, also in the role that I have at the university. It boils down to the attempt to answer the question: What is good, and what is right? What is fair for everyone in the moment, but in the system, in the process, in the knowledges, in the language registers, that continues consciousness of what is good and what is right? At least in my case, as measured against what in our country, especially in our constitution at least and so forth in various places, we say what is good and what is right. I know that's always broken. In my case at least, it is always broken, I think. But for me, practically, that's the thing. Whether it's in a meeting or with a student that doesn't have a place to sleep, or whether it's a policy process, or a plenary conversation or so on. But to ask what is good and right for the individual there, for the group, for our history, for our future.

I think the most difficult part of that conversation is to not repeat the patterns of our past. I find that to be a challenge. What I mean by that is to say that the most crude form of continued patterns, of course, are often argued by white students when you talk about employment equity and social justice, all of our restorative processes in response to social injustices. White students will argue and say, "I wasn't part of apartheid. I am from a new generation now. I have to sort of stand back for a black candidate when I'm on the same level of competence or capability or whatever." In a crude form, the argument is then made to say that we are continuing the patterns of some kind of injustice, which of course, is not the case, but that's their perception.

I give you that example, but on a much more fundamental process level, almost a community psychology level I would say, there's patterns continuing. For instance, how do I not *only* reflect on history? I have to decide who gets bursaries [scholarships] in the panel discussion. When I'm part of a panel discussion, and I have to very personally decide between a white and a black student, how do I not choose the black student in the face of the history of our country, but actually choose on the merits of the case in front of me? For me, that's a personal thing, but of course the point of panels would be to balance those of us that struggle with that personal conversation, those of us who might have progressed, had more experience of having that conversation internally.

But to me, when you talk about the practice, how you find expression for the injustices, the second part is how do we discontinue patterns or the fundamentals of it? How do I truly listen to the actual history of someone that sits in front of me and not my sense of the history and what we are to do with that? How do we not still fight the fights of the [liberation] struggle, pre 94, but now fight the fights of 20 years later? What's really the cause today as opposed to the cause yesterday? What should continue is our principled direction of what we believe to be good and right for our people, all our people.

JA: So there's a different objective reality now, post struggle, that has to inform your ethical judgments. You have to have a different horizon in terms of what encompasses and informs your ethical decision-making. It sounds like your ethical sensibility is really at the center of how you think about what you do as a leader.

RB: Definitely. Absolutely. I don't think there's another way to learn that, quite frankly, for me at least. I mean leaders make mistakes, always make mistakes. What I want from people that I follow is the attempt to do the right thing and the majority to recognize when you need to shift from what you're doing to continue to do the right thing. For me, it is core, absolutely.

There is a context for that. My placement in the history of the world today is here; tomorrow it might be elsewhere, but today it's here in this context, in our country, at a public institution, where we struggle with so many historical and current issues of people and how people are in the world and so on. You know, this is the context; this is South Africans. It's our dreams and our hopes; it's our history of aspirations. Our aspirations compete now, still do, and how younger and new generations' aspirations are translated from their parents' and other generations' and how all of these things talk to each other.

JA: How has your experience of the liberation struggle informed your understanding and practice of leadership for social justice?

RB: I'm trying to liberate myself from the liberation struggle! It's part of the pattern of conversation I've just had. I have the fortunate or unfortunate history of having grown up in a house that was part of left politics in the past. Growing up, you learn a certain way of gauging what at least you consider the injustices in society around you. Part of my own individual struggle is to not simply continue the patterns of struggle that I've been taught in our family and in the communities that I've been part of through that. The liberation struggle surely has a major impact. The paintings on my wall [in his office] are of struggle heroes, and it's on my wall because I value these people; there's a few missing here. Because they are the voices, they have been the voices in my mind. For the past few years I've begun to question myself, if I'm not simply repeating the voices and not actually fighting the struggle that's on the table.

I have a great appreciation for the Economic Freedom Fighters [a new revolutionary socialist political party led by Julius Malema, which received more than 6% of the vote in the 2014 national election], who at least in perception want claim a different struggle for a different time. But undoubtedly

58   *B.R. Rudi Buys*

it has influenced my direction, and so forth, and which voices I value and which voices I prefer to listen to. But I am quite conscious of it. I'm 40 now, so I'm quite distant from these generations. I'm also 15 years younger than most of my senior colleagues at the university, which means that I am part of a different generation that thinks differently around the liberation struggle and wish to continue what they really achieved, or not, through that. But I would sort of bring it down to that one point to say that I'm reflecting on how to disrupt the patterns of how we have sought freedom in the past and how we should be seeking freedom today.

JA: You talk about disrupting the patterns, the cultural practices, the epistemologies, all of the things that are embedded in the past. It's a whole different struggle in that sense.

RB: This is a big year for me because of this being 20 years after 1994. I was born in 1974, so I've lived 20 years with apartheid, and I've lived 20 years without apartheid. For me, this has been a very reflective year. Is it possible to compare? Is it possible to say what's different to life before and to life after 1994? In actual fact, that's why I say in some ways it's fortunate, in some ways not. That internal exposure to people and engaging with difference and so forth, through God's grace in life, and my family's life, not much has shifted in my life in terms of experiencing people. I've not grown up in my traditional ethnic community, for instance, and so forth. My own life has been one marked by diversity experiences over time. For me, it's for people to work out. But what has shifted is my parents' emotional responses when they see black and white students together. Because they grew up in a time where it was a struggle, and with no experiences of their own, it caused them harm. But, of course, I'm from the next generation, so it's very different. But to reflect on what's really different, you have to go deeper, of course.

JA: You grew up in a left-wing, progressive family context?

RB: My father is one of that group [that formed around Beyers Naudé, a leading Afrikaner minister in the Dutch Reformed Church and an outspoken critic and opponent of apartheid]. He was the next generation from Beyers Naudé. I'm also a minister in the Dutch Reformed Church, and my father, and so on. But my father had worked with black communities all the time, basically, but from the Dutch Reformed Church. I started my own ministry and congregation in the Free State in 2012. I was ordained with Beyers Naudé's gown as well, so it's that part of history. My parents had been church workers, if you will, and through that worked in the interdenominational church field and had been part of academic training and so forth in black communities from the 70s onwards. It wasn't party political; it was faith-based.

JA: Did you grow up in Namibia? How long did you live there before you moved to South Africa?

RB: Twenty years. I was born in 1974. At that time, my parents had been working at QwaQwa [a former black homeland in the eastern Free State province], at a school there, and a year after we moved to Namibia. I knew no other reality than Namibia. I grew up in northern Namibia and southern Namibia and so forth, living with my parents, and then I moved to Stellenbosch. I moved there in 1993, and since then I haven't moved back to Namibia.

JA: How did growing up in Namibia, in the context of a progressive, faith-based family experience, affect you?

RB: I remember at the missionary station, where my parents had moved to from South Africa, that when we would return after dark to home, we would drive slowly and stop, slowly and stop, as my parents would be checking for land mines on the road on our drive back to the missionary station. I grew up in the first five years of my life in a military sense of war. Apartheid wasn't far in that sense. We then moved to eastern Namibia, where the Khoisan community is, and they built schools there and so forth. Of course, that was also a military zone because the Khoisan community there had formed a unit of trackers. The Khoisan community, they're sort of the oldest people on the continent, but they're incredibly great trackers to track spoor and stuff, so that's also a military environment.

Then, of course, my parents moved to southern Namibia, where for the first time my parents actually worked with white communities, which was a tough experience because we had very different views. That had a huge influence on me. Of course, what is interesting today is that history doesn't shift the fact that I'm white, and male, and part of the Dutch Reform Church in a different country. Leadership for social justice, of a white male theologian from the Dutch Reformed Church, like Beyers Naudé and my father, meant something at the time; today it doesn't. If you lead the battles, you're not leading for social justice, as an example. It's a fascinating question to reflect on.

JA: We just talked about this a little bit, but how does your racial identity and your gender identity affect your understanding and practice of leadership for social justice?

RB: Before I started working here, I knew I was white, and male, and Afrikaans, and Christian, and Dutch Reformed – very strong labels that carry high emotional value and conflict. But I didn't understand how that makes me a perpetrator. Leading for social justice in Stellenbosch and the Western Cape was one thing in a context where white power, in reality and in perception, was dominant. I would assume it would be very similar to pre-1994 for Beyers Naudé. It's easy to then be progressive.

But then we moved to an environment where these labels are often still perceived to hold power, but in actual fact they don't. I think you discover what it means to become the perpetrator, to symbolically become *a* perpetrator or *the* perpetrator. In this context, when you ask about racial and gender identity, I must say that I've discovered, much more fundamentally then before in my life, how deep the injustices in society, based on gender and race, also in language and so forth, how deep the injustices are cut, and how incredibly deep the pain and scarring of our people are. In a very

60   B.R. Rudi Buys

real sense, in a very practical sense, what that implies for a dean of Student Affairs at an institution that at least tells itself that it's transforming and what it means to be a perpetrator.

JA: What does it mean to be a perpetrator?

RB: I'm trying to figure it out!

JA: Because I'm thinking how your position in society, your history, and how people see you. That must complicate your job enormously.

RB: In my case, I had moved to this institution after Reitz [the racial incident in which five black employees of the UFS were humiliated by four white students] as part of the intervention. My own self-definition in the role here, when I started out, and to my mind within this institution, was it needs change to resolve the racial conflict: That had been my self-definition. Four and a half years down the line, new colleagues have joined the institution with the same self-definition and have discovered, or have arrived with a sitting dean of Student Affairs, who is white, and male, and Christian Afrikaans, and Dutch Reformed, and therefore *must* be part of the establishment that we're attempting to transform.

That's one sort of dynamic that I've noted. In that dynamic, in that establishment, you are a perpetrator. When you act with authority, or you act with power, it is perceived not as conduct of change but as conduct of the establishment and sustaining the establishment. That has caused difficulty. There are a number of case studies that have taken place this year that would illustrate that. For instance, you would find that an executive decision to stop a certain Student Life program would not be read as an initiative for change but as an abuse of authority.

That, of course, causes immense difficulties. That's why I give so much attention to disrupting the patterns. I do think the patterns play a role when you're a younger colleague with senior colleagues: There's an intergenerational dynamic; it plays a role. Sometimes I would think: What's going on here? There's something happening between these people that is another conversation of a different time, that I'm not a part of. I would say that would be another area.

The other side of all this, in terms of race and gender, is something that I'm struggling with, and that is, the more the white male is fought, as part of the establishment, the more the white male becomes the white male, or at least is seen differently; the more difficult it becomes for the white male to deconstruct whiteness, to deconstruct masculinity and his own understanding of how to do his work and to live his life. The tougher it gets to change the project, almost strangely, it also forces upon me, again and again, the question: What am I? How male am I? But I think that's a good thing. It's part of the meaning and the cleaning and so forth. Because we are racialized, I'm racialized; it's just the reality, you know.

JA: I've been reading about the JBM Hertzog situation – you know the audiotape of the discussion is up on the Internet – and I listened to it several

Something much bigger 61

times. I thought you were incredibly respectful to the students in that conversation, but I know you've gotten a lot of flack from the Afrikaans media for what happened. I listened to the recording several times and pulled out a few things I wanted to ask you about because I thought you made some interesting statements.

You seem to be appealing to their better nature, or trying to, and had that difficult moment with one student not respecting you. I'd like to flesh out some of the things you talked about. In the discussion you say that we're all broken and traumatized people who make mistakes, who don't have all the wisdom. Can you talk about how this view informs your understanding and practice of leadership for social justice?

RB: I often think I'm too aware of brokenness. One of the most difficult things with this meeting, and then calling and the whole media response, was that it created the perception that this intervention is the start of something, when in actual fact it is at the end of something. Many of the methodologies and language in the recording that was circulated are the same approaches we have been using for three or four years in the Cultural Renewal Program [which is designed to transform the climate and cultural practices of residence halls] with all the residences. After three or four years, and there's no resolution of the conflicting situation, this thing follows. It's important to learn that. Otherwise, one would think that the positions taken in the recording is my position, or a new position, but in actual fact it's a position we've arrived at over time. We've enriched the program and how we reflect on it.

I always tell students: I will listen to the content of your argument; convince me, and I'll do my best to convince you. In practice, if I'm convinced I'm wrong, I recognize that because I'm broken. It's an unwritten expectation of anyone in leadership in general, but especially in our country, especially at our institution, where you're in leadership positions or when it's clearly faculty positions. But the point is that you can't lead at a senior level at this institution and not think it's about social justice and not think it's about reconciliation. How in the world can anyone in our country claim to not be broken in terms of those processes because the reality of our history, of centuries of history? If at any point anyone would claim different, it's simply a lie.

But what it does not take away is the fact that when a community gives you the authority to say you must run a process, at some point you must take the authority and decide. We can all make mistakes; we're broken. But at some point someone must voice what is good and what is right and stand up for it no matter what. Being broken does not take away the fact that you have to have the grit to run with the authority, to do what is good and right for all our people. The difficult thing, at least for myself, leading in this environment, is to never compromise on the fact that I've been entrusted by this community; by the alumni community, whether they like it or not; by parents; by founders; by whoever to take decisions about what is good and right for our students and good and right not only in the detail: Are the kids happy? In actual fact, the real, principled value of what is good and right in terms of our country, our history, of where we want to go – what is good for them to arrive at freedom. That boils down in my mind to process. Often the announcement of process is misjudged for the process itself, as in this case. In actual fact, what I was painting that evening was, if you will, the theoretical context, the language context, the process context, painting the first sort of frame of what it should become, this community, and then handing the process over to the students.

A comparative case is a case at another residence hall called *Vishuis* [Abraham Ficher Residence], with a tradition that they had called the *tikkie*, where women would be showered in the residence. They would organize a social between the men's and the women's residence, between the sorority and fraternity. The sorority would then come over, and they would shout the name, and then the guys would take them into the showers and shower them. Then the women have a choice: They can shower cold with their clothes on or with hot water but without their clothes. It's terrible; it's terrible.

We made various attempts over the past three or four years to work with a guy to change it, to stop it, to do something new, but nothing really works; it continues. Two weeks after the JBM announcement, I took an executive decision to say, "It stops now." Never again at this institution will that be there, with incredible anger, of course, from the students' side. My conversation with students was to say, "I will never shift my position on the matter. For me, it's a principled, ethical decision, that this is not right, and therefore, you cannot continue with that. But you can decide on what you design to put in its place, and I will give you financial support. If you need consultants, I'll organize the thing; I'll give you all the support. You decide and come to something new in line with our values, but this thing stops here."

The conversation back is, of course, the negotiation: How do we negotiate? It takes time to build the fundamental consensus on the values. I would tell students the following, I would say, "Listen, this will never change. Only for two things will this change; one, if the university fires me, if this decision is ethically, and principally, and consciously incorrect or, number two, you get me fired by negotiating elsewhere. But this is not going to change. There's only one other way in which I will leave this, and that is if I myself become convinced that my decision is ethically indefensible. If I have taken a wrong decision on this matter, I will resign myself." I've made that commitment to students, and I will honor that commitment to students if I have ethically made an incorrect decision.

That's how important it is for me to keep that integrity, that if I say I'm broken, but our attempt is always what is good and right. If I am myself convinced that I've done something unethical, I'll resign myself; I won't wait to get fired. I think if you're not prepared to so strongly defend a position, then you should not lead. But that's how serious I feel about this. But you can only do that if you really understand how broken you are. This is not a faith comment or a faith concept or terminology. It is really understanding that as humans, we are broken people; we are beings that attempt the good and the right. We are not the good and the right; we think the good and the right. On a fundamental human value basis, good and kind, a leader of people, but you make mistakes. But I feel very strongly about that. It is for me a core approach.

What I'm often critiqued for in the inner circle of my colleagues is that I say sorry too quickly. I apologize too quickly; I too quickly say I could have done it better. Because the general perception is if you say you're sorry, you're quite right, I could have done that better, then somehow you've given away some of your authority or your power. I apologize, but I really don't care about authority and power; it's not important. What counts is whether you're effecting change that is good for people. Whether students hate me or love me, whether staff hate me or love me, we've got to do things at this institution that will give freedom to students in a meaningful way, where they can have proud moments in their history and proud moments of overcoming their history – all of them, you know.

JA: Is that what you mean by greatness? I was intrigued by that because basically you invited the students in this discussion to participate in what you called the 'quest for greatness,' which requires that they be open to change. You appeal to students to open themselves to change, to work with you for their own sake. What does it mean to pursue greatness, and how does this inform your understanding and practice of leadership for social justice?

RB: For me, greatness starts with overcoming yourself. I will keep on saying *attempting* to overcome yourself because I'm not convinced you can really succeed with that: to attempt to just let go of yourself and reach for something much greater, something much bigger. We always sit with young people between 18 and 24, and most of them have their minds and experience of life in a completely different era than most of the rest of us at the university. Who can really drive change at this institution: us, staff? Over my dead body – students can drive it! But they don't see it; they don't get it, that the real freedom is not in my grasp. It's in their grasp. About what they're doing, they're choosing all my troubles from the past; they're repeating my nonsense. The test for greatness, I think, for this generation, is that attempt to just reach beyond yourself. If I get angry with Rudi, just be great and reach beyond it; just step over it and listen to the argument. Just try and build something, not for your past but for your future.

Greatness, for me, is about reaching to the beyond, if I have to give an analogy to that. Then to realize, without being theoretical in relation about it, but just realizing the things that my parents and their parents had dreamed about symbolically in our country. Everyone can have equal opportunity; everyone can have love and life for whoever they want, those basic moments and aspirations of people, of being human, that that can be true, the new sense of community.

64 *B.R. Rudi Buys*

In practical terms for residences, greatness is not a new tradition of power but actually a new custom of equal *recognition*, of shared decision-making, of open debate. All of those things that the students know, and that I know they want, holding themselves back. For me, greatness for them would be to reach: I can fight this now but let go of it and just reach out. With students you have to talk in practical terms and give examples of what greatness would look like. Of course, all this is intertwined with a social media space with the idol mythology: How do I become the next hero for whichever sort of community? But that's not my definition of greatness.

JA: So, for you, it's reaching beyond yourself, beyond your history, beyond your traumas, beyond your brokenness and trying to reach out to the future, to others, to a different reality.

RB: My point is just attempt because attempting is enough. Just the fact that one would attempt it really shifts your own sense and people around you, their sense of a new world being possible. In practical terms, let me give you an example; you might have picked this up in the media. Shortly after JBM and so forth, I arranged for Miss South Africa, who's one of our students, to go and visit JBM and *Vishuis*; I arranged breakfast for them. I invited the captain of the rugby team that had just won the national league. We never had a talk about it, but once they begin to associate with this process around values and aspirations, and then around how to give expression to that in our community, they begin to associate also the very practical sense of achievement of society at large.

Miss South Africa is not invited to anyone else. She was invited to speak to these guys because they're busy with a unique process. Of course, I might say that's a bit of a manipulation of the process, but the reality is that they get excited with Miss South Africa; they want their pictures with her put on Facebook and get excited. At the same time, they're also busy with this process, which is built around values and so forth. She enjoys being there because there's a different sense among the students. It takes a bit of time, but then the greatness gains a practical traction because students are seeing things that can become possible for them. But we need a critical team of leaders in the residences from the students' side.

What you would not finally talk about, in talking about greatness, is meaningful interracial contact between the students, and wonderful expressed engagement of difference, because these things are givens for me. A great community is one where everyone is welcome, where everyone has the confidence and safety to speak, where all opinions are welcome, where there's a difference of genres and sporting codes and so forth. The more diverse in all respects a community is for me, that's a great community. But for me, that's a given, that's part of what we're trying to do at this institution. It's not even a point of discussion for me. For me, the discussion is why people struggle to get there. For me, it's that very personal psychological-emotional process of not knowing how to or not wanting to reach beyond what is right in front

Something much bigger 65

of you. Because that reality of a diverse world of happiness and joy becomes possible, at least in our country, if individuals are able to reach beyond.

That's what I'm talking about, the differences, the social justice themes of a new community, because those things are givens to me. For me, the struggle, emotionally, psychologically, almost spiritually, I would say, is to reach beyond. For me, that then is the definition of greatness. Because otherwise it becomes a question: But why are we not talking about diversity? Why do you want to talk about that? It's not even a discussion! Don't waste my time with that discussion! I mean really, honestly, you know. In senior management it's the same. I mean, give me a break, all right, it's a given! In what country are you living?

JA: In the discussion at JBM you make a distinction between power and authority. You say that authority stems from greatness, not from one's social position or seniority. You argue that you gain authority not by control, structure, or military practices but by inspiring people to do great things through mentorship and inspiration. How does this view of authority inform your understanding and practice of leadership for social justice?

RB: In practice it means that the type of conversation and the emotional tone of the conversation that I have with individuals, with colleagues, with students, matters. That is where mentorship and inspiration take place. That's also where you test yourself in terms of your own confidence on issues of social justice: how confidently you are prepared to share your view on what is right and what is not and so forth. For me, it really starts with that care and how that care finds expression in the processes you design. Is there a process that a leadership team adopts that reflects on issues of workload for staff? Instead of presenting more training programs, rather present discussion forums on topical issues of interest that facilitate, not the technical training to spend less time on a job and therefore you have less load, but actually table issues of thinking and reflection and so forth because that's care. That's care.

For me, it's the program and process of reflection on the world of ideas, if you will – how that world of ideas communicates fundamental trust of people in who they are, that they reportedly contributed to the process of change, actually are drivers and cocreators of the process of change. On the other end, the very individual conversations that attempt to inspire. I'm authentic with people; you've got to know your own story to be able to have such conversations. You've got to have worked through your own narrative and have questioned your own narrative to have questioned who you are, how you have come to be, who you are to yourself, if you liked who you are, and be able to share from that story at the right point so that people connect. To be able to inspire and mentor and so forth.

For me, it doesn't boil down to a technical strategy of how to manage people. For me, it's really on that baseline fundamental level of whether you care for people. For me, one of the most difficult things is organizational politics; it's a huge struggle for me. Where there are moves for positioning,

66 B.R. Rudi Buys

and alliances, and all of these types of things, I find it very difficult to negotiate that. Because, for me, organizational politics fundamentally challenges an ethical principle attempt at how you lead, how you build community, how you build organization. It has its downside, if you will, an institution which is marked by organizational politics. Again, I say I don't think there's another way to live.

JA: You talked a little bit about this already, but perhaps you could flesh it out a little bit more. What are the greatest personal and institutional challenges to practicing leadership for social justice in higher education but specifically here at the UFS?

RB: I've learned that when you talk about leadership by individuals in senior management positions, one of the biggest challenges would be that people's own processes of dealing with history, and dealing with the traumas of history, those processes are at different points in maturity; healing and not is one of the main challenges that we have. It is generational; it is specific narratives of individuals; it is the combination of teams and individuals in teams; it is the interrelated environments of an institution, the different environments of more ready, and others are less ready, and all those normal institutional differences.

But it is fundamentally about individuals and teams, maturity of conversation around traumas from the past. That's why I would lead with the question, in my own definition at least, of what it means to be a perpetrator. A perpetrator's status has currency, politically and otherwise, at this institution but also nationally in our country. It plays into who can say what at what meeting, who can drive whichever change process, and who can drive at what speed and so forth. That's a major thing I've learned; that's an important jungle to find your way through for your own healing as well.

But I think that's a major one. The other major challenge is a legacy issue in academe from the British model of education where there's a very clear distinction between faculty life and the rest of your life, as if your engagement in research and your discipline is something separated from the actual world out there. I'm simplifying the definition, but that's a real dynamic. Of course, our attempt to breach that strategically by referring to the Academic and the Human Projects still shows that distinction.

For us, a major challenge is that when you work in Student Affairs, I know this is a global sort of frame, but the answers are considered to be within faculty. The responding practitioners are considered to be elsewhere, when in actual fact everyone is theorizing both the practice and the theory of what change should be. In our country, specifically, the hidden curriculum of life outside the classroom is terribly fractured and nonintegrated and nonintentional around transformation nationally.

At our institution, of course, we're attempting to shift that. It's a very conscious project for us. We try to create curriculum in Student Life that facilitates the process of change for students but consciously so. We evaluate all of that but not on the quality argument of what are good standards and good practices; that's one side of it. But on the fundamental pedagogical consideration of what is good and right. What is citizenship? What do students do with these things? The JBM case is a very important case study.

JA: It reminds me of one of your articles in the *Mail & Guardian*. In the piece, *Lectures Alone Are Not Enough* (Buys, February 14, 2014), you say that Student Affairs provides the space outside the varsity classroom where much of the broken spirit and lost opportunities of young people, commonly attributed to our schooling problems, can be and often already are restored. What do you mean by this, and how does this happen?

RB: That line I added later on to the original article. In a very practical sense I often sit with students, here or elsewhere, and hear their lack of confidence, their fundamental misunderstanding of their own value and their own potential, and their own ability to change the world – their world and our world. I really mean every word that I'm using here. Not only in a phenomenological sense of changing your world, and therefore the world is changing, but in the real sense of changing the life for yourself and for the people around you for the better.

I sit with them, and I see this incredible individual, and all of them are like that, all of them; it's incredible! But they don't see it, and worse, they don't believe it. It's a complex discussion, but in my mind that is due to the legacies of traumas, of historical traumas of families and communities and the society, and so forth, and how that layers and layers and layers in the lives and the thinking of our students. In a practical sense, it boils down to students thinking they won't get a job and in any case because they're black or they're white. Therefore, they're not giving their best in their studies, and then they fail. When they fail they say, yea typical, the establishment is failing me, or for whatever reason they are failing, and then they repeat the failure.

What do they repeat? They repeat the history we actually are trying to deconstruct. Well, that's my perspective. What we should be doing at varsity [at the university], in faculty and elsewhere, but OK, at least in Student Life, is about rekindling that moment of belief: I can do this; I can really do this! No matter how hungry I am, no matter how angry my parents are, and other people in the country, no matter what nonsense I have to go through on campus, for whatever reason, I can do this. That's what I mean by the broken spirits to be healed and the lost opportunities. For me, that's the level that it's on. I can't say this at the moment because our attempt in Student Affairs, in our institution at least, is really to build pathways on that level.

My test for our co-curriculum in varsity is not: Will they get the best career services at this point in time? The question is: Will the career services connect both with their fundamental belief of their value and who they are and, secondly, with opportunities where they can express that? That, for me, is really the test. Many universities do that already in different ways. But I

68   B.R. *Rudi Buys*

don't want to underestimate that, and that's not a black thing; it's not a white thing; it's a generational thing. How do these young people not live the life of their parents but live their own life in a free world?

JA: Obviously, your religious beliefs play a fundamental role in all of this. Can you talk about that a little bit more?

RB: I'm not one much for religious beliefs; I'm much more for spiritual identity. I draw a lot from the narratives I construct, and I'm constructing those responsibly to understand how I am, how I've come to be, basically in terms of what I do, behave, and so on. Also I have an effect on it. But for me, the spirituality that I live with draws mostly on examples of spiritual leaders that had lived counterintuitively, had lived counterculturally, had lived counter to what the religious establishment had argued for at the time. That is why I'm referencing Beyers Naudé and others, of course. Also, of course, a bit of my family and history that has positioned me in that way.

But I've also found a great inspiration in ancient traditions of spirituality: Christians in the environment from the Coptic Orthodox Church and from the Buddhist tradition as well. The symbolic language and symbols of a number of traditions, also within Islam, for instance, I find very interesting, the traditions and the language to draw on.

I prefer to go back many centuries rather than the immediate of where we're at, attempting to see what makes a world of symbols. It is through these traditions, and I question myself in terms of that religion or spirituality, that I seek the patterns of justice that continues beyond me and beyond my reality; that plays a role. I am incredibly irritated with the Christian churches in our environment. I am happy for the contribution that they're making, deracializing the young generation in some respects. But I'm essentially greatly irritated by the fact that the Christian church in our environment has not fundamentally shifted in messages on differences between people, and on equality of people, and on freedom of people. At the moment, the religious environment is more to my frustration.

JA: The kind of rhetoric in the diversity narrative or the tolerance narrative?

RB: Tolerance. Because I come from the fields, I understand why, I appreciate the positions. But in my faith perspective, as positioned as a Christian, my definition of the core dogma, if you will, of the cross and the resurrection, is that it breaks history and tradition and culture fundamentally, it's a complete shift. Even in the core fundamental beliefs that I hold within the Christian tradition, I believe that the Christianity that we are practicing mostly in this context, we're not realizing the fundamental meaning of what the cross and the resurrection and the Christian message in actual fact is. Irrespective of much of my approach to change, and my theory of change, that function, at least in my own mind, has to do with deconstructing and reconstructing.

You would have found that also in the messaging at the meeting at JBM, where I would talk about: You leave what is bad; you rethink what needs change; and you create new. It's the same with the ideology of deconstructing and reconstructing and so forth. But it comes from my fundamental understanding of faith that the cross breaks it and the resurrection creates something new, which has many of the old, but which is fundamentally new and different. One could also argue and say that defines, or that would explain, how the dean at some point can certainly make an executive decision to say the showering of women stops: If you don't like it, fire me.

Because it's from north to south, not from north to northeast. Because we've tried that, it doesn't work. Wrong, stop it! Right is shifted and redefined and so forth in new worlds. But I don't lead with my perspectives. I think it's important to know that also in your reflection on leadership for social justice. I was convinced that it's important to be able to share and speak from your own narrative, for the sake of authenticity, when you engage students and staff in the process of change because it requires authenticity.

But in this environment I've learned that the religious space is more sacred than any other in terms of its political currency. Therefore, if I share from my own experience of faith, it carries political currency: It is not read as authentic. That has been a huge lesson for me, to learn that no matter how authentic your take might be in sharing from a faith perspective, it carries almost only political currency in the environment of change in this institution, but I'm suspecting in the country as well. Don't say Jesus, say Jesus and struggle!

JA: Your training is in theology, and you're a practicing minister. You sort of have two hats that you're wearing now, one as a minister and one as the dean of Student Affairs. How do those two relate to each other?

RB: Spirituality is my foundational identity, not the only one but the most prominent, I would say. I think of the world through spirituality, maybe through faith; I'm not sure. I think it's rather spirituality would be more precise.

JA: How do you distinguish in your mind between spirituality and faith?

RB: Spirituality is a capacity of being human, is your sense of the bigger world, more than yourself, of other consciousnesses and other realities before and after and beyond you, the notion of the other, fundamentally in nature, in the cosmos. But also going inwardly, other consciousness, but at least psychologically the union of the world and so forth, the continuation of ideas and consciousness beyond myself. That is, I would say, my fundamental sense of process and pattern.

That's why I prefer the ancient traditions of religion and faith. Because of that, my core identity is not as dean of Student Affairs, or as an intellectual, or anything else; it is the attempt at making sense of the world, which I would define as spirituality. Within that, due to my historical placement in this world and in this reality, I have particular faith notions that is a collection and a compilation, a contested world of family and other histories and narratives of myself and people around me and so forth. To the best of my ability, I test these faith perceptions, and I hold them to be true in terms of

70 B.R. Rudi Buys

freedom and justice – basically, being fine in association in whichever tradition or notion. But because of that, to be a minister, and to be so in the Dutch Reformed Church, is an expression of the intersects of spirituality and history as it relates to my life. It was important for me to give expression to that moment and live it. Therefore, what I'm appointed to do here, and what I have given myself in this process, flows from spirituality and not the other way. It's not two hats; it's one being and finding expression in different points. That's how I make sense of it.

But what I'm very grateful for is that, differently so for Beyers Naudé and my father, and my mother, of course, but for the moment, is that in post-94 South Africa, in post-94 Dutch Reformed Church, I can speak the Beyers Naudé speak and remain a minister of a congregation, which holds very different views on these matters than I do: That's a difference of my generation.

I can be well-known at our Church synod, and so are the chairs, for supporting the Belhar confessional traumas of much of our history; apartheid churches where the white church, and the black and the colored and the Indian churches are the same family. The black and the Indian and the colored church at some point combined to form the United Reform Church and then adopted a new confession, the Belhar confession, that speaks about social justice.

For 20 years now there's been a discussion between United Reform Church (URF) and the Dutch Reformed Church (DRC) to unite. Uniting the reformed churches requires that this confession be adopted as a confession as well; it's a very current debate. I've been participating for 20 years in that, and my position is clear: I support Belhar in full. But at the synod last year, I would get up and say at the synod of the Free State, the region, and say I confess Belhar, and that would not lead to expulsion out of the community in that environment, emotionally. I'm not saying procedurally but emotionally: It's a very different world.

There are conflicts, of course, with human congregations, when things like JBM happen. I was called by the church council to come and explain what is happening – the fact that I'm a minister and was named in all the media reports. The Church feels it's becoming our struggle. It's a wonderful thing, of course. But we have one conversation, and then we have peace, and we are all on the same page, and the congregation supports me. The council supports me and tells the congregation that we support Rudi and give him all authority to continue with the work at the university. It's a different world in that respect, but it's not less tough emotionally because I know, and they know, I'm left and they're right, for argument's sake. But they hold it; they hold it. It's a great complement from the DRC, which is becoming, to my mind, in actual fact.

JA: You found a new home in the Church?

RB: Precisely. One of the biggest traumas for me of the past two months in leading for change at this institution is that my comrades have been silent when I

Something much bigger 71

needed support. Those that you would assume would not support me came out for the support. All of those white parent-generation, that in the popular perception of our institution are the enemy, were the ones who would call and say, "Rudi, listen, we know it's tough, but just keep on. We support you; we know you're doing the right thing" and so forth. My comrades within the institution that drives the program of change, with whom I drive as a matter of fact, were silent and showed no support.

The question is: Why is that? It's a difficult question, which I haven't been able to answer for myself. The discussion of organizational politics is simply not strong enough; something else is happening. I think it has to do with the question of who can drive change at what point in time. The stereotype labels that individuals respond to might not be the precise set of labels that we need to drive the change process; that's my early reading of that dynamic. That's why I say; I do think one of the biggest challenges to the change issue is the fact that different people view change from the different points of their own process of dealing with traumas from history.

JA: Obviously, you get a lot of resistance, and your spirituality has been a very significant factor in your identity and your ability to carry on. What are the things that keep you going when you go through tough times?

RB: My son, as you would read now my reflection on a family history as an access point to a reading of societal history. That's, of course, one way of looking at it. As you read from our discussion of disrupting patterns of conduct and trauma, and responses, and so forth, the question is: How do I honor my implied commitment to disrupt the patterns for my son? Not in the easy reference of saying, "But I'm here to create a better world so that my son can live in a better world." The fundamental one is to say, "When can I give up in the face of such an environment as we've come through the past few months? How much should I carry, fundamentally shift, the reality of who I am?"

My son, who's now a year and a half, is young. Not only the world out there but the world in here sends something different, sends some feeling. How can I be a different man? How can I be a different white man? How can I be a different white Christian man? A different white Christian Dutch Reformed Afrikaans man and so on? These things have to do with the attempt to move beyond, to reach beyond. I can't expect students to want to reach beyond if I'm not willing to attempt the same, if I'm not prepared to back up the role that somewhere needs change. I can't do that because then they can give up. Honestly, it's been very tough, very tough – no doubt about that. For me, it has to do with thinking through the baseline experience in my life, with my son presenting a very real experiential environment to assess whether change is possible. If I can succeed in this space, then possibly I can succeed also in changing who I am for my son to change, to live a different life.

That's one part of it. The other has been, of course, that I have drawn immensely on the support of family, and also I've drawn immensely on the support of being in nature; spending time with those things that remind me of the spirituality of who I am: seeing the craters on the moon with a telescope and reflecting on how incredibly wonderful that is, watching sci-fi movies to remind you of what is possible, that there's other worlds possible if you're willing to dream – you know, simple things. But also, I have an incredible team of people that I work with, who in their own right attempt to live inspirational lives, who would leave me a bunch of flowers and give me a call late at night and say, "You OK," who are equally upset with the convocation meeting [an assembly of primarily Afrikaner alumni in which Reverend Buys was vilified for his leadership regarding JBM], send letters to show their disgust with what our fathers do. I consider myself to be incredibly privileged, in actual fact, to have so many things to draw on during a tough time.

If you want to theorize change leadership, I would argue that the thing, at least in my life, at least in one case study, that has given me the most energy to continue is when students need to reach out to do the things beyond. For instance, if you sit with JBM's residence committee, the student leaders, and you sit with the SRC [the Student Representative Council is an elected body that represents the interests of students], some of the SRC members celebrated much of the change around the shower thing, and you see how they begin to sense how something different is possible, and we can actually do it. They begin to discover that, and begin to sense that among themselves, and then begin to step into that authority: Phew, that is energizing!

But the point is that you have to wait for it. It takes time, and you have to find ways of sustaining yourself until that comes. But, you know, I've not once taken the faith decision to trust students after a tough decision and have them not honor that, not once! Some have taken longer, some have taken less time to get there, but not once when I've pushed them and said, "This is right. Stop doing the wrong thing. I believe in you no matter what you think. You can do it; go and do it, but I will not have you cross this line." Not once have they not come up with something brilliant, not once. I think that draws me, always, that they can do it. Maybe what draws me then is if they can do it, I can also do it. Maybe that's the fundamental of it. If they can succeed in change, then possibly I can also succeed in change; maybe that's it.

Something that we've tested at campus here, and that has been shown to be true and precise, is really that when you set the bar high, now they reach it; every single student can do it. Before you set the bar, you have to sort of work with the students, not only in terms of getting your distinctions, practically, but really in being human. If you call on students for greatness, they will give it back to you, but you have to call for it; you have to demand it and not compromise on what is not great. What they need is for you, for me, to have the courage to stick to your position: "I'm not shifting guys. That is nonsense. You will stop with that, but I believe in you. You can do greater things." So come with it, and they will come! But you've got to expect it; you've got to want it; you've got to demand it and not compromise on the position that's the opposite – not once, every time. So I've been called an authoritarian.

Something much bigger   73

JA: I know you're a PhD candidate in higher education here at the UFS and that your research examines patterns of change in the race knowledge of university students in South Africa. What do you mean by race knowledge, and how does it inform your understanding of leadership for social justice?

RB: Intellectually, I draw most on Professor Jansen's work [Jonathan Jansen, vice chancellor and rector of the UFS and author of *Knowledge in the Blood*] on race knowledge. Basically it is about how a student's sense is racialized, is primarily defined by race and all the political notions around race and the psychological and other aspects of that. The way that I've operationalized it in the study is to try and trace how four students, who had played a counterintuitive or countercultural role in the racial dynamics on campus, made sense of the concept of race through their lives. What have been their core experiences, the critical incidents that had constructed their notion of race and therefore their knowledge of race itself? I attempted to find patterns between the life narratives, the life histories of the four students, to see if there is a pattern for change agents. My early or initial conclusion, but that's what I'm still working on, but I'll share with you, is that there are patterns between the students, between incidents and definitions and reflections they shared during the interviews.

But it seems what has shifted most prominently was not notions of race but knowledge, notions of knowledge. What had shifted most prominently was that generation of students had positioned themselves in the knowledge relationship and in relation to the university, not as subjects but as objects. The university could not change because, in our perspective as a university, we consider students as objects, full stop, and we still do, quite frankly.

The change project shifted through Professor Jansen's leadership around race. He made students subjects in the knowledge relationship at the institution regarding change. Suddenly students could be designers of knowledge and creators of process and the staff be equally broken and make mistakes, therefore the collective wisdom. The relationship that had been linear and hierarchical had shifted. What had happened, in actual fact, is that you had key drivers, key change leaders at the university. You had a rector and dean of Student Affairs in key positions in the arena where the crisis had been around race who had taken in individuals who did not consider students to be objects of knowledge. Therefore, the process of change, led by the environment at the institution, did not continue the process of a linear hierarchy of power and knowledge but established a horizontal model, a sort of sense at least, that would allow for different student leaders to step forward.

In the past, you would have protests on campus. Why? Because leaders called forth from the students' side by the leaders on the staff's side were leaders that responded to the bipolar tension: the conflicting relationship of those that know and those that don't know at the institution. While at the moment you had staff leaders that called forth cocreators, you had different leaders stepping forward that could translate the change project, that could facilitate the transition to a new environment. We have not had protests on campus since then. You could argue my thesis is about the reach for greatness, students that could reach beyond and do the exceptional. How could they do that? How could they reach beyond?

The interesting question for me in thinking about leadership for social justice is what seems to be the ebb and flow of growth at an institution. For instance, five years ago the university was ranked nationally 15th, for argument's sake; five years later the university is ranked at 12, for argument's sake – a huge jump in a short period of time. Suddenly, the type of programs, the national image, the international engagement, the scholarly seniority and so forth, the number of Fulbrights at the institution shifted, double the number of Fulbrights given to the institution, so that the quality of undergraduate students applying had increased and so forth. Suddenly, the stakes are higher. Quite separate too, or maybe directly involved with the change project, there's a greater political contestation for resources, for positions, for power, and so forth. A by-product for the authentic intent of the transformation project is higher stakes that people compete for.

That seems to, in actual fact, again, detract from the transformation project. The question that I would have, and I think it's important to reflect on, is how leadership for social justice causes this dynamic of building the new world but brings with it greater contestation, what you could argue would be the normal nature of any organization or institution. Is it possible to actually decrease the contestation as part of the transformation project, or is that just a by-product that you have to accept? Of course, I don't view that to be the case, but it seems that I might have the wrong end of the stick in terms of idealistically expecting that political contestation can be less when you succeed with transformation: It just might not be.

The one side to it is: Who would be the heroes of change? Which of the comrades would be more comradely? I'm really simplifying it. That would be one side of the contestation. The other side would be those that succeed with change gain power, perceived power, at least. Then there's more contestation for that power, which is not about the change project but about the power. Anyway, it's things I've noticed, and I think I'm affecting them. I haven't arrived at a conclusion, but that's a fascinating question for me.

There's one discussion point that you might want to also explore, and that is specifically the transformation project, the transformation of student politics and student governance at the university [the SRC adopted a new constitution in 2011 that forbade individuals participating in university elections to stand as representatives of political parties]. It's a very specific case study, which in our situation is very interesting. I think it's an interesting case study because it is an expression of how it shifted for the university to take a position to create a space for students, a new environment, and how that led to peace and not war. While at the time it was defined as, in actual fact, counterchange, counter-transformation, because it was doing away with the very thing that will bring us transformation, namely, political contestation.

But in actual fact it was fundamentally transformative because it shifted the institutional approach and required different engagement from students. When in practical terms, it is shifting the power dynamics so that the few don't decide but the many do – having the 25 students actively engaged in a political party speaking for the rest. We now have stabilized at the second-highest percentage of voter turnout in SRC elections in the country every year, and it's going up. Something is working, but we haven't decided. Who decided: They did! And what do they tell themselves? We decided! It's incredible!

Significance and implications

The notion of going beyond oneself, of reaching beyond one's identities, cultures, and horizon of experience is central to Reverend Buys's conception of leadership. His challenge to students and others to transcend the limits of their history is the same challenge he sets for himself. While we cannot completely escape from our sociocultural formation, and the discourses that produce our identities, we can nevertheless seek to know and critique who we have become. In a post-conflict nation like South Africa, where "the oppressed and oppressor are not as easily identified anymore," and where race continues to be a color line that deeply divides society, Reverend Buys argues for pushing back against social norms and cultural practices that undermine the possibility of solidarity in shaping our self-understanding and definition (Buys, 2015).

For him, good leadership requires that we acknowledge our brokenness, the fact that we will make mistakes, which makes it possible to arrive at better decisions. In his view, one of the primary tasks of educational leaders is to interrupt the patters of the past, of how people view and interact with one another, in order to fight the struggles of the present. In the end, Reverend Buys's leadership is driven by an overarching ethical commitment to do what is good and right, to help students see themselves as subjects rather than objects of history and university policies, and to recognize their own power to shape their lives and educational experiences.

References

Buys, B.R. (February 14, 2014). Lectures alone are not enough. *Mail & Guardian*. Retrieved from http://mg.co.za/article/2014–02–14-lectures-alone-are-not-enough

Buys, B.R. (October 27, 2014). *Taking it on faith the story of trusting you: A talk on the transformative power of spirituality in leading change in divided communities.* [Video]. TEDx UFS. Retrieved from https://www.youtube.com/watch?v=Mw94m7rQJzw

Buys, B.R. (March 27, 2015). I too, am Africa. *Mail & Guardian*. Retrieved from http://www.thoughtleader.co.za/rudibuys/2015/03/27/i-too-am-africa/

5 Repairing the brokenness of the past
Working through the unfinished business of trauma

Pumla Gobodo-Madikizela

Professor Pumla Gobodo-Madikizela is the South African National Research Foundation chair for Historical Trauma and Memory and Professor and chair of Research in Transformation at Stellenbosch University. From 2012 to 2015 she was senior research professor and director of the interdisciplinary program on trauma, forgiveness, and reconciliation at the UFS and was previously professor of psychology at the University of Cape Town.

Professor Gobodo-Madikizela is an internationally recognized expert on the transformation of individuals in the aftermath of mass trauma and violence. She is the author of numerous journal articles, books, and edited volumes, including *A Human Being Died That Night* (2003), which won the Alan Paton Award in South Africa and the Christopher Award in the United States, and has been translated into three languages. In the book, Professor Gobodo-Madikizela examines her conversations and interactions with Eugene de Kock, one of the most notorious killers of the apartheid regime, who at the time was incarcerated in Pretoria Central Prison, and explores her desire to understand how ordinary people can commit such heinous crimes. The text was adapted for the stage and premiered in London in 2014, and has been performed in Cape Town and New York.

Professor Gobodo-Madikizela grew up in Langa township in the Cape Flats area, near Cape Town. After being expelled from a private secondary school for African girls operated by the Baptist Church in the United States for promoting Black Consciousness among her peers, she earned a BA in psychology from the University of Fort Hare in 1977 and went on to earn an MA in clinical psychology from Rhodes University and a PhD in psychology from the University of Cape Town in 2000.

In 1994 Professor Gobodo-Madikizela was awarded a dissertation writing fellowship from Harvard University but interrupted her doctoral research to serve as a commissioner on the Human Rights Violations Committee of the Truth and Reconciliation Commission, where she coordinated the public hearings process in the Western Cape region for victims of the apartheid regime. When the commission completed its work in 1997, Professor Gobodo-Madikizela returned to the United States after receiving a peace fellowship from the Radcliff Institute for Advanced Study [Radcliffe College was renamed after it merged with Harvard

Repairing the brokeness of the past 77

University in 1999] to complete her research. She was also awarded fellowships from the Kennedy School of Government at Harvard University and the Harvard Divinity School.

Professor Gobodo-Madikizela led research teams to Rwanda and Germany to examine what it means for survivors and their descendants to live together with perpetrators in the aftermath of historical trauma. She has given numerous endowed lectures and keynote addresses on trauma and forgiveness in post-conflict societies and lectured at several universities in the United States.

Professor Gobodo-Madikizela has received many honors and awards, including being recognized as one of the '100 people who made a difference' in the Permanent Exhibit of the Hall of Heroes at the National Freedom Center in Cincinnati, Ohio. She also received the Eleanor Roosevelt Award and the Social Change Award for 'contributions made by leading psychologists in South Africa' and was named the 2016 Distinguished African Scholar at Cornell University.

The program in trauma, forgiveness, and reconciliation offers several postdoctoral fellowships and sponsors public lectures, conferences, and discussions. In 2015 the program received a 10 million rand grant (approximately 680 thousand U.S. dollars at the time) from the Andrew W. Mellon Foundation to fund a five-year research project that will examine how the arts and theater can provide a platform to engage the public and stimulate conversations about their experience of historical trauma; focusing on how trauma is transmitted to youth intergenerationally.

Professor Gobodo-Madikizela is also a public intellectual who seeks to spark and influence discussion about issues such as race and reconciliation, leadership and morality, and gender and violence against women. Some of her writings, which appeared in the *Washington Post*, the *New York Times, ThisDay*, the *Mail & Guardian*, and other publications, were collected into a book, *Dare We Hope?* (2014), which explores the unfinished business of historical trauma and social transformation in postapartheid South Africa.

Professor Gobodo-Madikizela has never been afraid to be a solitary voice or to stand alone on issues, if necessary, when important ethical principles are at stake. Her life is marked by an implacable resistance to all forms of oppression and domination, whether it means assisting women to leave abusive husbands, becoming an ANC activist in the liberation struggle, or exploring how victims and perpetrators of historical violence and trauma can live together.

Professor Gobodo-Madikizela (hereafter **PGM**) began our conversation by discussing how her work informs her understanding of leadership for transformation and social justice.

PGM: You know, I always think about it in the context of what we have gone through, all of these countries that have a history of historical trauma. I think that these countries need a particular kind of leadership because they're emerging from an era of gross human rights violations – just no human rights. These countries need a particular kind of leadership.

78   *Pumla Gobodo-Madikizela*

My sense of understanding of leadership for social justice is leadership that is concerned with transformation, with a very specific focus on how do you repair the brokenness of the past, how do you put into place structures and programs and relationships that will facilitate growth towards transformation in the aftermath of so much brokenness. It's about creating the environment for the repair of relationships, at the interpersonal level, the black–white interpersonal level – transformation within communities. That's where the brokenness happens. Leaders who embody a sense of care, a sense of empathy and connectedness for all these goals are the kind of leaders that are necessary.

JA: How does your understanding of leadership for social justice inform how you conceptualize and practice leadership at the UFS?

PGM: It's interesting. Whenever I hear similar kinds of questions, you almost have to think about what is it that you do. Sometimes you do things intuitively. But it's important, of course, to reflect on what is it that you actually do. Well, in a university environment there is the curriculum; there is the student body; there is the faculty body. Social justice encounters like ours, particularly at this university, involve so many levels that the key is how to bring people together from a history of separation, of regarding one another with suspicion.

For instance, at the faculty level, what's important is that people need to realize that we are now in a new era, and it's an era where we are building a different ethics. For me, it centers around the consciousness of a different ethical morality, at the core of this agenda for changing, for transformation. Leading wherever one can lead, wherever one does lead, in a spirit of refocusing people's attention on the thing that is new. The thing that is new now is that we have to think differently. We have to have a different kind of ethical core. In the past it was about those over there are different. Now it's different, and it's challenging for people who are used to a certain style of acting superior, of taking for granted certain liberties. Now they have to check themselves; and how do you do that?

The most important part of it is first of all developing and living this new ethical core and embodying it yourself. I believe, most importantly, is living by example – all these beliefs about where are we going and how we need to behave with one another. Whenever, for example, I'm involved in organizing something, I am conscious of how it's going to look, not only for the dressing of it but for its impact on others who are witnessing what I am organizing. For instance, you find a way of organizing an event in a way that different people can identify with different aspects of whatever it is that we are doing, from a simple thing such as who are the ushers of this event.

For instance, the annual reconciliation lecture – my staff here knows, for ushers I always say we must have a mixed race, women and men; it doesn't matter on the number, but it must have black and white. They must be represented so that students who come can see that this office is connected

Repairing the brokeness of the past 79

in reaching out to all these different people, the kinds of students and postdocs that I have. I don't advertise my postdocs, for instance. I go out of my way to find students in Rwanda, students in the United States, and not a big number but just so that they end up in South Africa. I tend to be concerned about ensuring that white students are represented because I am black. So in a way that's the dominant definition of the department.

The conversations with these students, with the postdocs, and with my students, are always about getting involved in projects that are about social justice. My PhD student, for example – in the first year of her study, I said, "It's always important to study, but do something once a week on a Friday; find something to do." She and a master's student went to a small community called Namibia Square; it's a small township that started after 1994. Now the extent of poverty is unbelievable. Because they are women, and because they are researchers on women and violence, gender violence, she started doing a focus group of just conversations about what women are going through, and that project has grown. Now we are involved in a major study on transformation because of what my students started, and it wasn't even their research. What this does is that it conveys a message to the others, whomever they're involved with, a message about the importance of consciousness, of reaching out and making a contribution to the community.

The second project, which the same students led, is the gender reconciliation dialogue. Samantha van Schalkwyk, who is my student, and Jessica Taylor, they led with inviting this group; and now that group is involved in negotiations with the dean of Student Affairs. That organization, the gender reconciliation organization, because of the initiative of my students it started in 2012, now they are in conversation with Rudi Buys [the former dean of Student Affairs] about bringing their services to bring consciousness about the importance of gender consciousness, among men especially, with all these tensions; and it's grown to a different level. That's the kind of leadership. I'm saying all these things because actually I'm just beginning to think about it, and that's how I engage with these issues – almost intuitively. It's almost like this is at the top of my mind; these are the things that I need to do. But most of the time there isn't a conscious plan, like now I'm going to do this and this. It's almost like this is who I am, and of course, this is what I need to do.

There are several things like that, and sometimes my students take the initiative themselves because of the conversations that we have with them, here with my students or outside. A few months ago I was invited by the SRC [Student Representative Council]. I have no contact with the SRC; I do not do work with them. They invited me to help mediate some tensions between them and the management, the student management body. I spent an evening facilitating dialogue with them. Again, it's an indication that, just that invitation by them, suggests to me that they know what this office is about. I asked the question: But there are other offices. There's

80   *Pumla Gobodo-Madikizela*

for instance the reconciliation office [the Institute for Reconciliation and Social Justice], which is the official body that deals with these kinds of issues. But they wanted me to help facilitate this conversation. I think it is an indication that, or a recognition rather, of something that this office offers – the way that you think and do things.

JA: I'm also interested in your philosophical, moral way of thinking about this. I'm wondering how the experiences you've had, both personal and professional, inform your understanding and practice of leadership for social justice. Were there important people; were there turning points; were there significant moments? What were the significant experiences in your life that led you to where you are today in terms of your leadership?

PGM: In high school I was involved in student activism, that is, in the 1960s, as a young student within the Black Consciousness Movement. I went to a private school for African girls. It was the only one in the country, run by an American missionary. It was called the American Mission Board. I think it was linked to the Baptist Church in the United States, one of the very few in South Africa, and were mostly in the KwaZulu-Natal area. The Inanda Seminary School was a private school for African girls. There was not a lot of freedom at this school but a kind of openness to allow students to express themselves, to think independently, particularly politically and so on.

The school's location in the wider Durban area meant that we were close to the heart of Black Consciousness conversations that took place at the medical school for blacks. Steve Biko and Dr. Mamphela Ramphele were students and leaders of the Black Consciousness Movement. As young high school students we were much inspired by this wave of Black Consciousness political activism of the South African Students' Organization [SASO was an all-black student organization that broke away from the multiracial National Union of South African Students in 1969 and emerged in the early 70s as a center of resistance to apartheid]. We were fortunate at our school because it was one of the very few that gave the student leaders of SASO a platform to address black high school students and to even organize some of the community-based projects that were led by SASO.

Some of the leaders who came to Inanda brought theater performance of plays that were banned in South Africa, but they could be performed secretly at Inanda. The first time I watched Athol Fugard's 'statement plays' such as *The Island* and *Sizwe Banzi Is Dead*, at Inanda as a young high school student, it was exhilarating to be part of that experience. I remember that the person who brought these plays to Inanda was Strini Moodley, who was SASO's founding member of the Theatre Council of Natal. We felt privileged to kind of have a front seat in the theater of the day that spoke back to apartheid. Inanda was also an important platform for the producers and performers of the plays, as one of the very few places where the 'statement plays' by Athol Fugard could be performed.

Repairing the brokeness of the past   81

The regular contact with SASO leaders also meant that we would know about performance events at the medical school, and I remember a few times when my friend and I would secretly leave the girls' hostel (residence) in order to listen in at a meeting of SASO. We particularly found it exciting to witness the women leaders, such as Dr. Mamphela Ramphele, in action addressing SASO. I count this early exposure to the Black Consciousness Movement as one of the greatest influences in my life, inspiring my own sense of leadership.

In terms of political awareness, that was kind of the springboard for me. Then I started working with some students, initiating some young Black Consciousness students. Of course, it earned me expulsion. One of the most loved principals was a woman. Her term ended, and then there was a very conservative man who came after her. In fact, that first year he came, an African American diplomat, his name was Charles Biggs, or something like that. He was invited by this principal, and the first thing he says is: "You are all a mass of faces for me. I can't make out who's different and who's who." That was the kind of ethos that he brought, and it earned me an expulsion, but not before I experienced another important turning point.

What I wanted to say about that is that I was the only one who was expelled; I felt very proud. The reason for my expulsion is that I was involved in a strike at the school because of the harshness; things had changed, and it was very harsh. This principal brought new rules, and there was a strike. I was, of course, identified as one of the leaders. They wanted me to tell on the other leaders, but I didn't want to do that. So that for me has been a sense of pride; I did not do that. I did not inform on others, and it was an important turning point. I was involved in a role of leadership, and I was not about to sell out the other students, so I was expelled. I was the only one expelled in the entire history of the school.

That was an important moment for me. It was in the middle of the year, and we were about to write matric [the high school graduation exam]. I was in the grade just before the final year, so I had six months to think, and to fret, and think about what this all means. All it left me with was a sense of pride, that I had maintained a role of leadership because of what I believed in and moved to another school.

It was also very enabling, although he said, "No politics here." At the same time, he allowed a different kind of growth, and there I directed a play, my first play, "Sir Thomas Moore." For me, even that, being enabled to direct a play on Sir Thomas Moore, it was very much about the principles that I believe. It's interesting because I didn't even think about the connection with what I believed in until much later, when I had to write a life story and so on, my inaugural professorship [at the University of Cape Town]. Then it clicked that this was a connection, of course, and the principal, by encouraging me to do this, and giving me all the funding, the resources to set this up, he was encouraging me in a different way – not kind of cutting off my vision and my ambition to be involved in this kind of leadership but enabling me. So that was a very important connection for me.

Then there is another important one that is very relevant to the kind of work that I do today. The year before my expulsion at this school, there was a group of white women from the Anglican Church. They started what they called at the time encounter groups. I really think they were just ahead of their time because that was what we would call today either diversity training or reconciliation groups and so on. I mean this is in the 60s, you know. I went to high school in 1968 and 1969, so it must have been in 1970. They brought us, my school, which is a private African girl's school, together with a white girl's school in Amanzanduti, in the Durban KwaZulu-Natal area. They just started; there was no agenda. We were just told we're going to meet the other school, and they would bring us together on a Saturday with no program, nothing, just allowing us to have conversations together and have lunches and teas and whatever.

That taught me a lot because when we came together, it was very unusual. We were like: What are we going to do with these white girls, you know? I'm sure they were also asking the same question. For me, it's the touchstone; that experience is the touchstone of all the work that I believe in. Because of what that did, it exposed me to the possibility that you can actually engage with people. That engagement opens up the space for you to connect with them, not as black and white, but as fellow human beings. In this sense we were young people.

These women were really very wise; they knew what they were doing. Because what evolved in all these conversations about boyfriends, about parents, about fashion at the time, I mean all these kinds of things that are girl talk, *that* really collapsed the differences in a literal sense – collapsed them. We would look forward to these conversations and be joyful about meeting. Of course, we couldn't maintain the relationships because there's no way we could go to where they live or them come. We had pen pals; we maintained a pen pal relationship. Of course, with time, after matric you go to university; it dissipates. But that was a very important turning point for me because it created an experience of awareness and a kind of teaching one about the importance of intentionality about these things.

These were some of the early influences. Of course, having the opportunities that I had in places like the Truth and Reconciliation Commission (TRC), for instance, and being the only black student in a master's class at Rhodes University, and weathering all of these challenges at a white university. Being the only black student, you are challenged. You can either be angry or you can try to understand and, painful as it is, very gently move things in a direction that you may not even be consciously aware of. That's what I learned in my years at Rhodes University. Part of the time I was very angry, but part of the time I was very reflective, having had that experience at high school, growing from that experience, the insights from those conversations.

Repairing the brokeness of the past 83

As a result, in fact, I spoke to one of the lecturers, encouraging him to start a group dialogue, just with us as the classmates; and that was very helpful. It's those things like and the Truth and Reconciliation Commission, and working side by side with Archbishop [Desmond] Tutu, and being able to use some of the insights from my life's experiences to understand how to bring people together.

I was leading the Human Rights Violation Committee in the Cape Town area. Often family members of victims wanted to meet the perpetrators. That experience both exposed me to the ravages of trauma and, at the same time, to the power of dialogue as a tool of reparation after brokenness. Again, it was another layer and several other experiences. Being in the United States for instance, and having the opportunity, almost to be an ambassador in a way, for the kinds of things, of learnings, that I gained from working on the TRC. Being given the opportunity and resources by Radcliffe [Radcliffe Institute for Advanced Study, part of Harvard University], where I was, to lead with conversations, whether it's in lectures or presenting talks in the Boston area and beyond, all of those experiences made me resolve in a way that this is right – the kind of sense that this is the right path; this is the right thing.

JA: This is a good segue into one of the questions I wanted to ask you. In your book, *A Human Being Died That Night*, you tell the story of when you were five years old and witnessed traumatic scenes of violence in Langa township, near Cape Town, where you grew up. You say that this experience left an indelible mark in your memory, which returned in a flash when you learned about the Soweto uprising [in 1976 black students were brutally repressed by police for protesting against the imposition of Afrikaans as a language of instruction] and the violence perpetrated by the police. Does this lived memory of trauma, despite the fact that it wasn't completely accurate, which you discuss, inform your thinking?

PGM: I think it's one of my life's experiences; it's not directly related to my sense of leadership. However, because it's all of me, I'm all of these things. It's an experience that marked me, a kind of awareness that people have been wounded in some way. Whether it is a real memory, in fact, I still think that sometimes, even if memories are not necessarily factual, they are real in the sense that they *live* as real. People who have had traumatic experiences, there's a woundedness that they carry with them. Having gone through that experience myself and understanding its impact in my life, later in my life, and how it spurred me on to engage in a particular action, then this prepares me for understanding. For instance, since I came to the university, I've been interested in what sort of impact the Anglo-Boer War [1899–1902 in which the Afrikaner republics were defeated by the British] has had on the survivors, on the children of survivors. What is the impact of that experience of suffering on the third and fourth generation?

Let me share with you another anecdote that's going to demonstrate this sense of awareness and how it works. When I served on the Truth and Reconciliation Commission, there was a very clear understanding, a set of principles in terms of who was considered to be a victim and who was considered to be a perpetrator. Victims were people who had suffered gross violations of human rights. One of the goals of the commission was to give as complete a picture as possible of the violations that happened in the past. My argument to the commission was: Well, if you want a complete picture, then we have to look also into what happened to the young white men who were forced to fight apartheid's war.

There was a huge debate in the TRC; people were angry at me. How can you even consider giving voice to young men who had fought in the army? But I felt very strongly that these young men, it was not so much their choice; the issue of choice is complicated. The parents who lost their sons in Namibia, Mozambique, wherever they were, they live with the wounds that no one has acknowledged because they're supposed to be heroes and so on; they should not complain.

I sort of pushed this idea that we should hear them. I'm not calling them victims necessarily, but I'm saying let's consider what their feelings are. What were the traumas that they were exposed to? Fortunately, the Archbishop [Desmond Tutu, who chaired the TRC] and Alex Boraine, who was his deputy, they kind of stood behind me, that this is the right thing to do. We just needed to find a way of making people understand at the Truth Commission. In the end, there was a very grudging kind of understanding. But at the same time, in the wider community out there, there was a protest, particularly among an organization of white women who felt that the soldiers had to go to the Amnesty Commission [one of three committees that comprised the TRC]. They almost messed us up, actually, because by that time I drafted this memo that was going to go out through the press that we're inviting these young men. It was along the lines that former soldiers of the South African Defense Force who experienced trauma as a result of participating in the army and those for whom this was a positive experience, so we opened it up that way.

These women, they were up in arms: These soldiers should go and confess to the commission because they're murderers and so on. Then I had to go and plead with a priest at the time, Peter Storey, who was a very respected man, a priest of the Methodist Church and recognized for his own activism as a leader of his Church. Peter Storey was the one to send out this memo to the press because these women had spoken to him. I then went to him and got him to understand what our goal was and why we wanted these men to come to the commission. We wanted to create a special hearing. It was agreed; now let's have a special hearing. It was called the Special Hearing on Conscripts.

That process, to cut a long story short, it was very moving. Even when I chaired that event, we got tons and tons of submissions from people who

Repairing the brokeness of the past   85

had escaped; they were fugitives. They left the country to avoid going into the army and to avoid imprisonment because they would be imprisoned if they didn't want to go into the army and suffer other kinds of humiliation – men who were fugitives in these countries, reams and reams. It was just at the beginning of, I guess, e-mail at the time. They were sending faxes, papers of submissions.

When I checked the special hearing, one of the things I agreed with my colleagues about is: Let's handpick the people who are going to sit on the panel. The way we structured the hearing, we made it into like an embrace, a holding. We organized the chairs in a very particular way because we were aware that these men are obviously anxious because they had killed people and they had participated in apartheid's war. They had killed their own citizens, some of them in the townships. We wanted to create a kind of holding environment that was visually holding by organizing the chairs in a particular way so that we would sit, almost like in a semicircle, then kind of catching them as they sat in front to close the circle. It was a very moving event. Wilhelm Verwoerd was my closest partner on this; he served on the Truth Commission. He played and continues to play an interesting leadership role in terms of transformation and change. He worked in the research division of the Truth Commission. He and I ended up being the co-organizers of the special hearing.

That is an indication then of how another experience, not only the experience of my young days as a five-year-old, contributed to my understanding of what it means to be wounded – subsequent experiences as well. Growing up under apartheid is a wounding experience itself; I carry all these memories because I know what it means to suffer pain and I know what it is to carry the memory of pain. It informs this kind of project, for example, the conscripts' special hearing. Being aware that there are mothers out there who are in pain because their children had died in a war. They were told lies basically, that they're fighting to stop people coming from outside the borders; they were actually in those countries fighting the liberation movement.

Some white people really did not know. Obviously, many of them kind of knew, but they were in a comfort zone and didn't really want to question things: It's complicated. My awareness, then, of the history of trauma has made these kinds of projects that I'm involved in possible. Because it's an awareness of the effect, of the woundedness of another, even another who is different from me. That's how I think I can make the connection.

JA: You talk a lot about brokenness in your writings in different ways, the brokenness of perpetrators. You also talk about the brokenness brought about by traumatic experiences in the lives of victims and the brokenness of the country itself. What do you mean by this?

PGM: Trauma causes a rupture. It disrupts relationships; it disrupts hearts; it disrupts the culture. Fortunately, these days we no longer look at trauma as an individual experience, as an experience that only affects individual victims. Trauma causes rupture in the culture. What I mean by that is there is a certain mode of understanding within groups in terms of how we relate to one another. There are certain things that . . . You just can't cross that line. There's like a line: This you can do but not beyond that line.

The beautiful statement that I can share with you is from a woman. I was in Rwanda in April. My research in Rwanda is also pursuing these questions: What was the effect of this? Talking to them about the brokenness of culture, I asked this group of women: How would they define brokenness within the culture? This woman says: You know, in our culture, when you're a mother or a grown woman within an extended family, there's a certain dress form. They wear like a cloth around their waist; it's not a skirt, but it's a wraparound. They hold this wraparound skirt with . . . Let's call it a belt.

When something happens in a home, let us say the man is violent, or whatever discord within the family, and they are intervening. The women don't always intervene, but when they intervene, their form of intervention is taking these belts and putting, almost like standing between the person and whatever acts they're about to commit, and putting their belts on the floor as an indication that now, you are going to cross a line. In the culture, you can't as a man, or anyone else, but especially as a man, that belt, you dare not cross because you are violating a culture.

Now she said to me that during the genocide, that didn't help. Sometimes mothers of the killers, of the Hutu young men who would want to kill their neighbor, the neighbor they've lived with all these years, and now they want to use what they know in the culture works. But that didn't work anymore. That, for her, and for me listening to it, is a powerful indication, not only in terms of the actual physical object on the ground but also its metaphoric significance: These men crossed the line. When there's brokenness within the culture, there are these lines that now are crossed left, right, and center.

I mean here in South Africa, for instance, just the notion of *ubuntu*. There's an understanding among most black people that *ubuntu*, your humanity, which is the connection to other people, the other person, your humanity depends on the other. But not only that, you are also responsible for bestowing the humanity, the humanness, on the other person; you have a responsibility. What that means then is that you *extend* your humanness towards the other in order to help them to become human again; that is the cultural understanding.

A few weeks ago I was in Cape Town. I was invited to be an expert witness on vigilante violence, which is to say car violence, in one of the townships in Cape Town: Khayelitsha township. I don't know whether you know about the Khayelitsha Commission. It's a special commission that was set up by the Western Cape provincial government to look into problems of policing in the townships and especially in Khayelitsha. I was one of the experts, and my role was to give expert testimony on crowd violence.

Repairing the brokeness of the past 87

This is not just crowd violence: People murder; they kill. You know why they kill? A thief who is caught stealing a women's handbag, they snatch a handbag or a cell phone, or break into someone's home. All the victim of the crime has to do is to shout, "Thief!" Everyone comes out of their doors; they just open automatically like that, and they descend upon this person. You will not believe the stories I heard. In no time a person could be killed, could die, could be killed in five minutes, with whatever there is: stones, bricks. People are killed just for stealing a handbag, a cell phone. You ask the question: Where is that old principle of care for the other? Some of these victims, well, they're victims of the killings now; some of them are young. You know, in the olden days an older person catches the young person, calls them to the side or even calls a small committee about their behavior. Now it has exceeded all expectations of what *ubuntu* is about in many of our areas, so that's the brokenness.

Of course, one has to understand what brought it to that level. But set that aside for a moment, and just focus on what do we mean when we say brokenness; it's those kinds of things. You know, when I grew up in the township, that word reliance really meant something. You rely on another. You rely on another for a range of things, from just making sure that my child comes home; and there is no fear. Now there's a fear; you can't trust anyone. You can't leave your child; even that is brokenness. You can't leave your child with a neighbor because you don't know what's going to happen. The neighbor may leave; there might be another friend of the neighbor who rapes your child. You know, these kinds of things never happened before. But now there is this discord within communities, and that comes with this kind of brokenness, this rupture of the core principles, the cultural principles that held a community together; they're no longer there. Some of them are more specific than others. But if you look, just on the surface, when you look at what is going on, just the news that you get from some of these communities, it's clear that the connection that we relied on, that human connection, no longer exists in many of these communities. That is the brokenness of culture, the cultural brokenness.

Then there's the woundedness of the self, which we cannot separate, of course, from the brokenness because those cultural bonds also equal those human bonds within the community – trust of your community, the trust that has been built among members of a certain street, for example, of a certain community. Where there's a deep sense of woundedness, loss, people lose the trust in others; they lose the connection to others. These are all related, these experiences of rupture, whether at the individual level, cultural, or community level.

Within the country itself, it's huge. We take lightly the importance of upright leaders. I think in our country, especially after Nelson Mandela, the general population take lightly the important power of an upright leader: We don't have it anymore. I write about it [in *Dare We Hope?*], this loss, this brokenness, this loss of a moral core at the level of leadership.

Because it's not visible; it doesn't trickle down. What trickles down is the negative value associated with this really tragic sense of leadership and the brokenness of moral leadership in our country.

JA: It's obvious from what you've said, and the stories that you've told, that both your racial identity and your gender are significant in terms of informing your understanding and practice of leadership. Could you talk about that?

PGM: We are what we are because of who we are. For me, as a woman in South Africa, I divorced the year after I got married. At that time, I was working as a psychologist in one of the bigger towns in the Eastern Cape, Umtata [the capital of Transkei, a homeland created for blacks under apartheid, which was renamed Mthatha]. After my divorce, I saw women who were struggling, who were struggling to leave their husbands, struggling to leave their marriages, or thinking that they depend on these husbands. Some of these women, in fact, most of them, were professional women; they didn't really depend on these husbands.

At the same time, in my early stages of practice, my early years of practice as a psychologist, there was also a big event. I mean I call it an event deliberately in the United States because these were the years in which Clarence Thomas [who was nominated for the U.S. Supreme Court] and Anita Hill [an attorney and law school professor who charged him with sexual harassment as a witness in the confirmation hearings], the publicity of that issue. This was the early days again here of CNN [Cable News Network]. Women were affected by these debates, by the debate that had become a global debate now.

For them, it evoked stories of being abused. I mean, although the Anita Hill story was not tragically traumatic in the way that you understand trauma, it was still an experience by a woman who was disempowered at the time, and it evoked so much. I was really surprised by this. I saw in my practice women who had been abused from an early stage, who had never talked about it, by uncles, brothers, their husbands, as well as these women who were struggling to leave their marriages. That was probably the beginning of my consciousness about the weight upon women's shoulders, of what it means to be a woman.

Then, of course, again, later on when working on the TRC and being one of the people who recognized the importance of us creating a space for women to testify, separate from the general space of the public hearings of the Human Rights Violations Committee. I then almost became a courier of these memories and of these stories. In my work, in various ways, I have also been a kind of witness to women's stories. Of course, reading helps because then you realize that this is all over the world; women are carrying this burden all over the world. Because women like me are in positions of some level of authority, through our writings and through our place within the community as professional women, we have a responsibility, in whatever way we can, not to forget there are women who are voiceless, even

Repairing the brokeness of the past 89

if they do have a voice but they are not able to have the reach that other women have because of our positioning as professional women who have an awareness of these issues.

Even in my op-ed writings, for instance, during Thabo Mbeki's years [as president of South Africa from 1999–2009], I wrote op-ed pieces about the importance of criticizing what was happening in the country because of Thabo's refusal to admit that something was wrong and needed to be done about the rate of AIDS/HIV infection. Then he made comments about women, about beating women and so on. Once he was on the campaign trail and he made a kind of joke, I suppose, from his perspective – something about beating a sister if he found out she was gay or something like that: I was very angry. I wrote an op-ed piece about what that statement means coming from a leader, a person in a position of leadership, and what it means for women who are beaten by their partners every day; here he is legitimizing this kind of behavior.

Actually it's a sense of responsibility as a woman. In fact, even when I came to this university, I was amazed and shocked that there wasn't any conversation about gender equality at all. There was a lot of talk about race issues – nothing really, almost nothing about gender issues. My group of active students, they again started a conversation on gender; the first one they had it at the institute [Institute for Reconciliation and Social Justice]. They partnered with a woman who was a lecturer within the Program on Gender [in the African Studies Department] and started these conversations, which went on for some time at the institute and culminated in an important international conference organized by one of my students. We funded it through my office and brought women from an organization, *Abahlali Basemjondolo*, whose name literally means 'the squatter camp dwellers' in Cape Town, a very active organization campaigning for the rights of the squatter camp dwellers. Their homes are demolished almost on a weekly basis and the way they have to survive with young children, giving birth under the most dire conditions.

We invited a group of activist women from as far as Cape Town and two gender activist–scholars from the United States. It was a successful event. Samantha van Schalkwyk and I are coauthoring a book on gender research (Gobodo-Madikizela & Schalkwyk, 2016). It's that kind of responsibility because as a scholar I always have to bring the scholarship side of things in all my work. My work straddles the kind of social consciousness and the scholarship. It's not always easy to do that, but I can't do it any other way. It's about responsiveness, a sense of the issues related to women's experiences and their suffering and giving voice to some of their experiences; that's the gender connection.

JA: I remember the story you tell in *A Human Being Died That Night* about an incident that happened during apartheid when an officer in the South African Defense Force who was leading a coup attempt against the leader

90 *Pumla Gobodo-Madikizela*

of Transkei was captured and killed. After the coup attempt failed you were driving around in a car with soldiers celebrating and you suddenly realized what had just happened, that you had participated in an incident that led to the killing of another human being. I'm wondering, how does your experience of the liberation struggle inform your understanding and practice of leadership for social justice? You talked about how you were influenced by the Black Consciousness Movement in high school and how that opened your mind in certain ways. Could you talk about how your experience of the liberation movement influenced your thinking?

PGM: As black people in South Africa, it's difficult not to be involved on some level. Of course, people are involved in different ways. For me, there are certain instances that I can share because I think what I said so far demonstrates how my life is connected to my positioning here, how my professional position and leadership is connected to these experiences. But perhaps to identify one or two instances that show the kind of role I played during the liberation movement. By that time I was at the University of Fort Hare and involved because there's an awareness that something has to change, and you cannot but participate; you have a role to play in whatever way you play the role.

There are two specific issues that I want to share. One relates to the years when I was at Fort Hare. As students, there were moments where there would be strikes; there would be periods where you would strike; there would be student meetings and student bodies where you have to take a decision: Do we leave; do we stay? For me, whatever was against the system was the right thing. However, I loved education; I wasn't one of the people who didn't want to have an education; I wasn't one of the people who campaigned for no education. On the contrary, I was very clear that if I have to lose a year, I wanted to come back next year to finish; I don't want to abandon education and not study. I was very clear that I wanted to have an education.

There were two years, successively, we had to leave university. There are always people who are against living on principle. My principle was always: This is the right thing to do, supporting the struggle against apartheid. One instance was when I left to come to Langa [the township in the Cape Flats area near Cape Town where she grew up]. I think it was the first time I left the university and came back the following year. That year was lost, lost in terms of I did not get my credits for that year.

And then another year, where I spent that year trying to go to Lusaka [the capital of Zambia, where the ANC had military training camps]. I wanted to go to Lusaka. But there was a much older man; he was very quiet, a quiet kind of activism. In fact, I think that he was even past his retirement. He was connected to the struggle, people in the struggle abroad and in Lusaka especially, and was helping those of us who wanted to go to Lusaka. But I was clear; I didn't want to join the MK [*Umkhonto we Sizwe*, which is Zulu for 'Spear of the Nation,' the armed wing of the

Repairing the brokeness of the past 91

ANC]; I didn't want to fight for the ANC. I wanted to be in the wave of thinking, to go to the university there and study but be in Lusaka. I was about to complete my honors, and I wanted to go and do my master's. He was engineering all of that, was helping me with applications and so on because I wanted to go to Lusaka. For me, it was the idea of them [the ANC] being there and being in the spirit and the heat of the conversations about liberation. That was the end of my year, so I went home.

I was communicating with a man, Mr. Ncapayi, who was already there, who happened to be from my own hometown, who was based in Lusaka as one of the activists who had left the country. He was my main correspondent, the person who was helping me set up the scholarship to study in Lusaka. I went home that December, a holiday. Things were supposed to be finalized in December, so I was waiting expectantly. I was wondering why it wasn't happening. The holiday was moving along, and I was getting concerned. Then suddenly the police came to take me from my home for interrogation. They drove me from my hometown. My parents by then were in the Eastern Cape, in a small town called Cala. I was picked up and driven to another town about half an hour from Cala, Lady Frere, and interrogated for hours.

I was shocked. How did they know about my attempts to go to Lusaka? I was questioned about all of this for hours, and they wanted to establish whether I was a kind of conduit based in South Africa because some people of my age were involved as conduits in terms of arms and cashes and so on – planting firearms and communiques in different ways. I think they were convinced that I was not an armed person. I was interested in going to study, although I wanted to be connected to the liberation struggle. But my goal was not to fight; I wanted to be in that atmosphere. It turned out that the mail was intercepted. The postal services people themselves were working, obviously, with the security; that's where they intercepted the mail. They are the ones who could see this is from Lusaka, so they intercepted all the mail. That's why it never reached me; it was opened before it could even reach me.

That was one. Of course, I had to give up that effort, and I registered for my master's at Fort Hare, which was the year I would have gone to Lusaka. But there was another outbreak of protests at that time, and I said: This is it; I'm leaving. I already had my social work degree and my honors in psychology. I went to look for a job, and then I went to work as a social worker, first at the hospital in Umtata, and then I was moved to the rural area of Maluti [in the Eastern Cape], very close to Lesotho.

When I arrived [in Maluti] I knew no one; I had no family, no friends, no connection. But my parents knew the Njongwe family. Dr. Njongwe was one of the founding members of the ANC. By now he had passed on, but his daughter, now a doctor, had taken over the father's practice. My parents found me a temporary home with them, and I became friends with her. When I found my own place in Maluti, she brought me close to what was going on in terms of people that she would see as a doctor who were connected historically to the ANC. These would be people who are passing through secretly to cross the borders. That border was the safest, the small border to Lesotho.

As a social worker I got a team of people who developed false passports and false IDs for these young activists. Remember this is the 80s, and this is the period where many young people escaped. The first wave was just after 1976, the first wave of people leaving the country. The second wave was in the early 1980s, from 1982. As a social worker then, in 82 and 83, I worked with a group of people in the government office to develop false passports for these young people; that was part of my role at the time.

Someone within the network of police got wind of the fact that I was involved in this; I don't know how it happened. We had meetings in my home. This is a rural area and the small homes; it's easy to see, to kind of smell if something is going on. This was now the Transkei government at the time [one of 10 'independent' homelands created for blacks under apartheid], but they were working hand in hand with all security issues. There was a state of emergency in South Africa, and that extended to the Transkei. We had all these group meetings and numbers of people. We were caught again and arrested because of the meeting in my home. Again, I was imprisoned and questioned and so on. Of course, I had to protect these people who were the actual ones responsible for the passports.

As a social worker, I would write the letters to say this was a person in need of this, whatever the reason, and pass it to them. But they knew we were in cahoots, you know. It was a wonderful time, really, because when I think about that, and I think about the corruption today, at the time it was not corruption; it was doing something subversive but clearly for a good cause. And it gives me a sense of pride even to think about what we did then. We were arrested and spent a weekend; we were released because there was nothing that they could find.

I sued the minister of police, and that was another point of pride, that I will sue the minister of police. This is what happens when you are arrested for something that is unclear; you sue the minister of police. The other people, they were afraid for their jobs; they didn't want to do a civil suit. I was the only one who sued the minister of police. It's a very interesting story because the only lawyer we could use was a man called Leo Mtshizana, who was furnished by the Transkei government in Maluti. He couldn't go anywhere else; he had to be in Maluti, so he became my lawyer. Because the case was in the Supreme Court in Umtata, he couldn't go. In fact, that's how I met my former husband, the marriage that I had. He was the cousin of Prince Madikizela, a known ANC lawyer, a struggle lawyer. There were these kinds of human rights lawyers, and he was one of them. He represented me, and I won the case; I won 5,000 rand. I didn't know what to do with the money; it was a lot of money in those days, so I gave the check to my father, and he bought me my first car!

Significance and implications

Professor Gobodo-Madikizela argues that countries that emerge from a long history of gross human rights violations, like South Africa, need a particular kind of leadership that can create the conditions "for the emergence of forgiveness" required to "reanimate the empathic sensibilities damaged by violence between individuals and within communities" (2008, p. 173), that is, leaders who can foster an environment in which the brokenness in interpersonal relationships, communities, and cultures can be repaired. This means creating programs and institutional structures that cultivate relationships of empathy, caring, and human connectedness.

For her, "working through the unfinished business of trauma" not only requires that issues of economic justice and other problems be addressed, and the creation of public spaces that make empathy, remorse, and forgiveness possible, but that South Africans embrace "an alternative way of remembering the past" that does not perpetuate "the most destructive aspects of memory," such as revenge and retribution, and a "new public discourse that is imbued with moral possibilities and a sense of responsible citizenship" (2008, p. 169; 2014, p. 125).

References

Gobodo-Madikizela, P. (2003/2013). *A human being died that night: A story of forgiveness.* Cape Town: David Philip Publishers.

Gobodo-Madikizela, P. (2008). Trauma, forgiveness and the witnessing dance: Making public spaces intimate. *Journal of Analytical Psychology,* 53, 169–188.

Gobodo-Madikizela, P. (2014). *Dare we hope? Facing our past to find a new future.* Cape Town: NB Publishers.

Gobodo-Madikizela, P. & Schalkwyk, S. (2016). *A reflexive inquiry into gender research: Towards a new paradigm of knowledge production and exploring new frontiers of gender research in Southern Africa.* Cambridge: Cambridge Scholars Publishing.

6 There is nobody innocent here

Shared complicity and the sharp edge of social justice

André Keet

Professor André Keet is director of the Institute for Reconciliation and Social Justice and a member of the Faculty of Education at the UFS. After receiving his teacher qualification from the University of the Western Cape in 1986, he taught geography at Cloetesville High School in Stellenbosch. Professor Keet went on to earn an MEd in research methodology (cum laude) from the University of the Western Cape in 1995 and a PhD in education management, law, and policy from the University of Pretoria in 2007. He grew up in Kylemore in the Stellenbosch region.

After the new democratic dispensation in 1994, Professor Keet worked at various independent public institutions that were responsible for navigating the transitional phase of South Africa's contemporary history, focusing on processes aimed at deepening democracy and the promotion and protection of human rights. He joined the South African Human Rights Commission (SAHRC) in 1996, was appointed director of the National Centre for Human Rights Education and Training in 2000, and was selected by the minister of education to head the Human Rights and Inclusivity task teams, which were charged with developing National Curriculum Statements for the General Education and Training and Further Education and Training programs.

Professor Keet has also worked in various other capacities, including as director and professor of the Transdisciplinary Program at the University of Fort Hare and as deputy CEO of the SAHRC, and was appointed by President Thabo Mbeki to serve as a commissioner on the Commission for Gender Equality. In 2013, Professor Keet was selected by the minister of higher education and training to serve on the Oversight Committee on the Transformation of South African Universities, which monitors progress toward transformation.

In July 2011 Professor Keet became the first director of the Institute for Reconciliation and Social Justice (IRSJ), which was created in the aftermath of the Reitz incident in which four white students humiliated five black employees of the university. The institute serves as a space for conducting research and facilitating critical conversations about institutional transformation and human rights and sponsors lectures, conferences, colloquia, and discussions. It also houses a Human Rights Desk, which was created as part of the Reitz settlement, to promote and protect human rights, and serves as an ombudsman to resolve possible violations of human rights. The institute also offers postgraduate programs in reconciliation and social cohesion.

For Professor Keet, the concept of leadership is itself a contested term that he does not accept without qualification and would not use to frame discussions about transformation and social justice. In his view, changing the institutional culture of the UFS is less an issue of leadership, understood in the traditional sense of leaders who envision change and inspire others to carry it out, than of how to cultivate and instantiate normative values and practices within an inclusive, participatory, and deliberative context that can drive positive change at the university.

Professor Keet (hereafter **AK**) began our conversation by explaining his objections to using the term 'leadership' to describe how he thinks about transformation.

AK: I'm very ambiguous when it comes to the concept of leadership itself. I don't think that it's productive to keep on thinking in these terms. What I found, at the University of the Free State and in the rest of South Africa, is that it's a very hard currency, as a notion, an idea, and I clearly see how it plays out – the value that it brings. But I would probably use the term 'transformative citizenship.' That would be what I have in mind as a framing notion: transformative citizenship rather than transformative leadership. If you ask me what I mean by transformative citizenship, I would say that it's an everyday vocation of building solidarities for social justice work, a form of leadership, of driving the institution for purposes of advancing access and quality.

JA: How does the notion of transformative citizenship inform your work? We'll bracket the term 'leadership,' for now because it's a problematic concept for you.

AK: Professor Jansen [Jonathan Jansen, the vice chancellor and rector of the UFS] is doing a kind of leadership that I appreciate. He actuates the kind of leadership I would have in mind, but at the same time it is overstated as leadership in public discourses. I actually think that the kind of high-level discourse on leadership can sometimes be a bit overstated: That's the thing that concerns me. Because then you also set up people in terms of not developing ownership and ethical responsibilities in their own spheres of influence around various kinds of projects. Such leadership can be highly effectual if it inscribes within itself its own critique, its own shortcomings. You have to be very careful as to how you play that particular discourse and what are the pros and cons of that decision. I think the way in which one drives a process, as a discourse, it can be overstated. Leadership in the conventional sense can dislocate ownership of the process from the responsibilities that the whole university community should carry.

JA: How would you describe your approach to this kind of leadership?

AK: I would not even think of my approach as a leadership approach. I would simply look at myself as a person who occupies a strategic position that can contribute to driving different kinds of changes within the institute. That's

96 *André Keet*

precisely where the issue of leadership becomes even more complicated for me: It can be productive and counterproductive for the proper educational project. I understand that, for pragmatic reasons, institutions cannot do without certain forms of leadership. For me, it is not the idea that certain strong kinds of leadership are needed that can drive change; it's that the overexpression in discourse and practical demonstration can bring out a number of disadvantages. For me, it's the overstatement of that discourse, the leadership discourse, the mentoring discourse, those kinds of discourses. Once you overstate them, you bring out all of their disadvantages. You have to be very careful within leadership spaces; leaders should know when to lead and when to step back.

JA: I was just reading some of your work, and it seems like it's more focused on transforming social norms, transforming normative values. What is it about Professor Jansen's leadership that you see as useful or effective?

AK: I think Professor Jansen may present himself as a leadership type of person, if you write that word in capital letters. But he is more of a good, effective academic citizen than a leader in terms of his ability to inspire the university community and higher education sector. He is a change agent; a motivator or steward; a shrewd, clever academic citizen. Because he's so great at being an academic citizen, that's why he can drive us. He attracts his critics and has blind spots, as is the case with all leaders.

JA: What do you mean when you say he's a great academic citizen?

AK: I think he likes the fact that higher education spaces are there for students. That's his whole philosophy, providing decent learning and valuable educational spaces for students, of course, giving his staff various kinds of spaces too. He undoubtedly has the education of students foremost in his mind, the broadening of access for people of all backgrounds.

JA: How is that related to the formation of normative values at the university?

AK: The normative values must first and foremost have empirical counterparts that are observable within the university community. It must be something you can see before you can even start abstracting it. Of course, the authority we claim for ourselves is that we came to the normative values first, as to what students should be, without looking at what is empirically expressed, and are at risk of developing management practices at odds with the expectations of students. The normative values that are developed in those kinds of ways are more or less inaccurate and disjointed from reality when it comes to what students express politically as young people in the university community.

One of the things that's always been fascinating for me is, if you look at our young people, are the forms of expression they bring to the university. Instead of overlaying normative values on top of that, the normative values must evolve the other way around. These things that we're fighting for – solid academic work from students, decent behaviors, inclusive stuff – they're there empirically; you can see it. Of course, there are problems. But as soon as you abstract, say, for instance, one of the university's values into those kinds of spaces, you must make sure it has a counterpart that is already observable; otherwise, it can't be done. Students require a form of justice that recognizes their voices, social identities, histories, aspirations, and ways of engaging with the world and should have a strong say in formulating the terms of their recognition.

JA: Otherwise you're just transposing values on a situation that doesn't reflect them.

AK: Part of our studies here [at the IRSJ] are precisely to try and find out what those intuitive understandings from the students' side are, to explore their terms of recognition and what they see as the challenges facing the university and facing themselves.

JA: I want to switch gears here and talk about some experiences that may have influenced your thinking. Did the liberation struggle inform your understanding and practice of transformative citizenship?

AK: I grew up politically in the 80s, which was a very important period in my life when it comes to politics. The 80s, especially during my time at the University of the Western Cape (UWC), was a big school in many kinds of ways. But I was not a leader in protest politics, more of a committed participant. Apart from the 80s as a decade, the city of Johannesburg was the second-best teacher. I was fortunate that life took a chance on me and my family. Some great mentors awaited me in Jo'burg after leaving the Western Cape in 1994. I started working at the South African Human Rights Commission (SAHRC) and other public institutions in 1996.

The first time you really engage with Jo'burg, the world becomes a different place. You're in the city where there's no forced boundaries; everything is fluid. That was in the mid-90s. The kind of work I was doing certainly had a huge impact on my life. Of course, in the university context it was very clear the way in which one has to deal with substantive matters. You see, my predominant frame of viewing the world is that of politics. If the question would be, how does your politics, as you were socialized in the 80s and 90s influence you, I would say greatly so. I can trace my approach to social questions through the political in that period.

JA: Could you elaborate a little?

AK: I think most of the values that undergird transformation, the tools you are working with, standing up for justice, the way you look at things, have a massive impact. A social justice orientation towards one's life and work does not just fall out of the sky; it requires substantive work on the self and support from family and friends, all the support you can get. The 80s in Jo'burg provided that kind of assistance for me.

JA: Were you involved in the student boycotts in the 80s?

AK: Yes, but not as a leader. In fact, those kinds of things are still clear in my head. We had massive civil boycotts. I was a founding member of the South African Democratic Teachers Union.

98 *André Keet*

JA: What did you teach? I saw you were a secondary school teacher for 10 years.

AK: Geography. Environmental justice was one of my big areas of interest. I was first an activist in that particular field before shifting toward human rights, not that you can separate the two.

JA: So your entry into politics was through environmental justice.

AK: Yes, because it dovetailed with my work as a teacher. You have teachers, students, education, and politics all merged together in the 80s; boundaries between them were very fluid. We were working at that time already with the ideology. Environmental discussions were blurred into one big project: to get society to a point where we can actually say we're shifting.

JA: Does your racialized identity affect your understanding and practice of leadership?

AK: I'd say definitely because it's constructed independent of me but structures me. That is a function of history and the construction of racialized identities. The fact that one looks at the student in a different kind of way, looks at young people, it's hugely influenced by racialized identities and the experiences that come with that.

JA: You went to the University of the Western Cape (UWC) as an undergraduate. I am interested in how that experience of being racialized, of having a racialized identity within the context of the apartheid state, how that experience might have informed your thinking.

AK: The link is very pronounced, especially if you read my intellectual work. I'm trying to find a particular theoretical ground of shared complicity without losing the sharp edge of social justice. The one that works with shared complicity, which is in the making all the time, is how to retain that sharp edge but at the same time work towards social cohesion. On the other hand, as you've noticed at the university, the social reason discourse can mask so many other things.

Racialization is an instance for social justice work. Before and after 1994 in South Africa it is probably the unconscious starting point from which one works. The critical space at the UWC gave me useful tools to challenge my racialized identity, which is a lifelong vocation, a place to work on myself and against the system.

The idea of shared complicity entered my consciousness from the profound empirical reality that history is messy, that the concepts of perpetrators, victims, beneficiaries, and bystanders only serve a useful purpose in history up to a point. There comes a time when they become more complex, more empirically true. At this point, one begins to view the present from the vantage point of shared complicities, *not* equal complicities. The historical distribution of complicity is differential and asymmetrical; it touches us all. It would be foolhardy to think of a human subject entirely innocent throughout history.

Shared complicities gives social justice work sharper tools. As a racialized body, which I do not accept, my desire for a little space where one can have a messy and complicit history in the present, so that a possible future can emerge, is a way of giving my social justice work a sharper edge while also moderating it, if this tension can be tolerated.

There is nobody innocent here 99

JA: You talk about mutual vulnerabilities, and you say that you're not looking for a kind of equal vulnerability, like a cultural pluralism model, but for a recreated kind of vulnerability in which everybody more or less shares a new space. What do you mean by that, and what does it look like in practice?

AK: I have found it very strange that people wanted to read equal vulnerabilities. They see the word 'mutual vulnerabilities,' but they read 'equal.' This is the standard criticism I get from lazy readings. People see the word 'mutual' but want to read 'equal' to set up their critique – unfairly I think. Of course, I don't think we did enough in the mutual vulnerabilities paper (Keet, Zinn, & Porteus, 2009) to make that distinction. In fact, that's the piece I get the most hits on, citations on. It taught me a lot about it. It also sharpened those frames as well. When I speak about the issue of mutual vulnerability, at that time I didn't think of it as strangeness or making yourself a stranger; I didn't have those codes in my head.

In essence, mutual vulnerability speaks of a critical consciousness in which the act of social engagement demands a keen awareness of how the cultural codes in a given situation create asymmetrical relations of power. The codes serve some and work against others. The burden of self-consciousness requires a willingness to suspend codes that are taken for granted by agents to be vulnerable within their own cultural spaces. The burden must be distributed equitably so that one can give up those codes from which one derives power, to reconstruct a kind of strangeness from one's own familiar context, so that aspects of one's codes: the words, idioms, and sayings that one is accustomed to are revealed in the construction of power relations. This kind of vulnerability, of self-consciousness, is a burdensome condition. When it is shared, one can speak of a kind of mutual vulnerability, which is a key element of cultural justice.

You see, when I enter a space where my codes are present, it must not create a position of non-vulnerability for me, which is actually what people do because when their codes are present, they do not have a sense of vulnerability. I think of it the other way around. Precisely because it's present, I have to work hard to maintain a form of vulnerability given the fact that the power structures around you support you. In that power, you will have to make yourself vulnerable.

There are many examples of this. If you come with me where I grew up [Kylemore in the Stellenbosch region], there will be a number of terms and words that you wouldn't understand; the same would be for me. My responsibility would be to assist carrying your vulnerability since those codes are absent from your cultural makeup; I must almost act *as if* it's also absent from my own. That's the new spaces I had in mind, where different sets of vulnerabilities emerge because you let go of codes that are familiar to you and from which you derive power. Of course, a space of non-vulnerability, I actually think it's an antieducational space; you can't learn in a space without mutual vulnerability.

The Zimbabwean theoretician [Chirevo V. Kwenda was a professor in the Department of Religious Studies at the University of Cape Town] that I used for that paper was actually what I had in mind. You see, because if you come

100 *André Keet*

into my space, you carry a burden of self-consciousness that's much heavier than the one that I'm carrying. Mutual vulnerability means *me bending down with you to help you carry that burden*; that's actually what it means.

JA: I understand why some people misunderstood because in the United States, everything is filtered through the discourse of diversity and multicultural education, which is often about cultural pluralism. It's a very different discourse that you're using, but it gets translated into something else. I want to switch gears here and ask if religious beliefs inform your work. I noticed in your dissertation that you mention God in the acknowledgements.

AK: I'm a believer.

JA: Can I ask what church you belong to?

AK: I'm historically from the 'colored' *Nederduits Gereformeerde Kerk* mission church, now under the United Reformed Church in Southern Africa. I am from the most conservative church in the country, which in the past was very traditional and justified apartheid on religious grounds; that has changed now. I belong to the church, and I'm very loyal. I had some good ministers as well that you could actually talk to about life, that you can see struggling from the pulpit.

JA: Did those people play a significant role in your upbringing, in your development?

AK: I'm not sure, but its influence on my life is undeniable. As a youngster, you know, in primary school and secondary school, the Church played a huge role in socializing me in ethics but in favor of apartheid logics, of course. I'm fully aware of those because I was socialized in the process, and the racism of the Church plays itself out in some of my own racial prejudices. Of course, it functioned in a real firm, stark, strong, hierarchical way; you can't describe it any other way than a relation of colonialism that I've gone through. But I didn't leave the Church; I stayed in the Church and see myself as a critical member. Nevertheless, I am acutely aware of how the Church fed into my own racial prejudices as a colonial project. But the Church was also a source of social justice orientations, a counter-hegemonic force.

JA: Despite its complicity in the apartheid state, you managed to keep your faith in the DRC?

AK: Thinking about Christianity and, of course, about religion broadly today, I'm able to do that. People are so surprised when they find out. I say no: These contradictions I live happily with; I don't have a problem with it at all. It's part of my heritage; it's my mother tongue. You will regard it as the language of the oppressor, but I regard it as the language of liberation. Of course, in social justice circles I am constantly in arguments around my position. I am aware of these contradictions but am happy to live with them. I am happy in the sense that if one takes religion to its authentic kernel, one finds elements of justice there.

Because the UDF [the United Democratic Front was a national coalition of organizations formed in 1983 to coordinate internal opposition to

There is nobody innocent here 101

apartheid and create a democratic South Africa] struggle in the Western Cape was done in the language of Afrikaans, I don't have any desire for political correctness when it comes to those things; I've never experienced it like that.

JA: How does your understanding of transformation inform your work at the UFS? What does that look like in practice?

AK: I do not have a particular understanding of transformation but a range of constantly changing understandings of equity and redress. I see a shift towards more inclusive institutional cultures, a complete overhaul of what we teach, and the reconstruction of knowledge as part of the transformational agenda. But we have to start somewhere. Practically speaking, my work centers on facilitating engagement, so a new self-constructed ontology of the students emerges that has traction for changing management and education practices and initiates shifts in the social structure of the academy. A big chunk of my research is invested in this question.

Transformation would include all those processes aimed at redress, equity, and quality that advance them in the space of a university. If the university just does what it is supposed to be doing, which is teaching, learning, research, and community engagement, it would already be transformational. Of course inclusivity features strongly in my conception of transformation, but don't get caught up in simplified versions of transformation that only look at equity. Look at the diversification of knowledge, and teaching, and learning practices; that would be a much deeper form of transformation for me than getting the numbers right.

For me, one of the first areas is to review the ontological scheme of young people. I have seen it so many times. The image of the students that's presented within the space of the university is the body that must be regulated. I actually think that management requires the construction of a regulated body as one of the easiest forms. It's easy; you do it with your workers, with all kinds. Once you get that particular ontological frame out of your head and you reconstitute it, and that should be educational, all your other management things change. Then you can speak about dynamic management instead of regulated management. The issue of parameters is very important; the vision of the student that we have, that is the problem.

JA: More like what happens in classrooms with good teachers. You start from where the students are at; you don't just impose a curriculum on students that has nothing meaningful to them in it or doesn't in any way respond or relate to their own experience. Do you see it more in terms of reciprocity, a space where what students bring to the university, and what the university wants, gets negotiated?

AJ: It's not only what they bring; it's *who* they bring as well. That's my question. That's why it's an ontological one. It's who they bring, and we get the 'who' wrong in terms of their ontological makeup.

JA: Could you elaborate on that a bit? What goes wrong?

102 *André Keet*

AK: The imagined student is engrained in the entire operations of the university, of a regulated body to be disciplined by the academic disciplines. Many students know how to play the game, and throughputs [graduation rates] are not bad, but it's questionable whether this is critical education. The university also diffuses patterns of recognition and misrecognition that generally reproduce social inequalities. It is less that the university must be more inclusive and equalizing than an awareness of how the university prescribes the 'who' that shall achieve: The normative manages the nonnormative.

A student that comes into the university space is screened and constructed as the regulated body: It's classical Foucauldian [the French philosopher Michel Foucault] governmentality. Of course, there can be some good things coming out of it; power is not always bad, but we don't understand the mechanisms by which we construct students, so our self-analysis and self-constructions are outside the purview of our reflection.

JA: Like the overemphasis on leadership, too much focus on one particular part of the equation.

AK: Yes, it will be difficult to get to that point where you will be able to make substantive shifts in the university because the question of the 'who' is not being answered, or you might have a problematic view of the particular student.

JA: I want to flesh this out in terms of the specific challenges you've had here at UFS. What are the greatest personal and institutional challenges to your work, to driving the university in the direction you would like to see it go?

AK: Let me start with the institutional. At that level, of course, the institutional culture would be a huge constraining factor but also a facilitator. With the institutional culture, I more or less define it for my own purposes, not simply as the import of various norms and assumptions and frames about how the world works into the people you call an institution.

I regard it as more than a set of values and behaviors that are co-constructed via the core functions of the university. My notion of the institutional culture wouldn't be something that overlays an organization but something that draws from below the organization's foundations into its various policies, and practices, and so on. In that sense, within the three major mandates of the university – research, teaching, and learning and community engagement – reside the three major producers of institutional culture. If you get to a point where you define the institutional culture as conservative, or exclusionary, or racist, or discriminatory, or in whatever way, then you define the expression of its core mandates. A question would be: What are the norms and values that are generated and affirmed via knowledge, research, teaching, and so on?

In the case of say the recent racial incident on the campus [in which two male Afrikaner students were accused, and later exonerated, of attempting to run over a black student with a vehicle while he was walking on the campus], they are a function of our research, and our teaching and learning practices, as much as they are a function of the imported values that students bring to the university from home, from church, from all the other institutions in society. There's a massive interplay between them. For me, that is the *major* challenge.

Personally, I like working in the trenches, so it would be difficult to think of a personal challenge apart from the fact that it can take massive amounts of emotional energy. That's probably the biggest challenge: the time you have to spend on it. But the fact that this is a space where I knew when I came here that this is going to be the challenge, I don't mind that at all.

JA: So it's really about generating normative values from the ground up as a way to change the institutional culture. Could you talk about the kind of resistance you encounter and how your response is informed by your understanding of transformative citizenship?

AK: I encounter resistance all over these spaces, institutional and personal, but I also get lots of support. They balance one another and play out in many ways. The social reality, in any case, is probably meant to be like that.

I would probably employ three kinds of responses to these forms of resistance. One would be to try to understand better the institution and its dynamics. It's very time-consuming work over a long period of time, building your interpretative resources. My default position is to occupy a more conciliatory space where you try to deal with those resistances. It would be first to get myself up to a level of interpretative capital that allows me to make sense of the space in an informed and conscious way and choosing forms of discussion and conciliatory approaches over more combative ones, which may come later. The third approach, a weak strategy, would be to engage with resistances through institutional compliance measures – performance management and all those kinds of things.

JA: The constant negotiation between the conciliatory and what you call the sharp edge of social justice, and trying to walk that tension, that tightrope – given the fact that you obviously face a lot of resistance in your work, for various reasons and at various levels, what keeps you going? What are the personal resources, or ideas, or relationships that you draw on to sustain yourself in this long march toward a more equitable and just university and society?

AK: I don't think my work is exceptional or special or even frame it in the discourse of exceptionalism. Once you do that you've undercut so many of your resources already. It must be something which meets social reality in a way where you can clearly connect that this is a country-wide challenge in the 23 higher education institutions [There were only 23 public universities at the time of the interview, three more have been subsequently added].

One's resources are built through networks of collegiality and by developing interpretative and analytical schemes. We are facing a sector-wide problem around transformation on a national and global level. Go to some place like Mississippi [a former Confederate state in the Deep South of the U.S.].

104 *André Keet*

You read the reports now, and the UK, the higher education sector, then you see the global challenge. That's the first thing. You have many networks you can draw energy from in that particular space. But, of course, the thing that drives me the most is my pursuit in trying to understand social dynamics better. I do find great joy out of the intellectual project itself as an energizer. But, of course, you require networks of friends and colleagues, and I've got loads of them. I also have these different networks of international institutions, which we are closely connected to, and draw immense energy from young people, including my own children, in my pursuit to understand better the social dynamics of higher education institutions.

JA: I want to go back a moment. You talked about participating in the school boycotts in the 1980s, that you were a founding member of the South African Democratic Teachers Union, and that your entry into politics was through environmental concerns. So I'm wondering, was your intellectual development and conception of transformational citizenship informed by the Black Consciousness Movement?

AK: I wouldn't say yes. It would probably be more accurate to say that I engaged with Black Consciousness through the politics of the United Democratic Front, which included the Black Consciousness Movement. There were eclectic progressive political forces at play in one's political consciousness. I would not regard myself as a scholar of the Black Consciousness Movement; I would not regard myself as an active participant in those kinds of thinking spaces. Nevertheless, it's a conceptual framework that I'm comfortable working with; I don't have a problem with that; I subscribe to its major tenets. But in real, practical political terms, it was within the spaces of a broad democratic movement in the 1980s [the UDF], which included the Black Consciousness Movement but many others as well. One might say, if you want to frame it as a broad antiapartheid spectrum that formed, that was the defining framework which started in the early 80s. Of course, being privileged to be at the University of the Western Cape gave you depth and substantive tools and intellectual orientations to sharpen up your political consciousness; that's how it just worked out. You're at a university that actually provides schemes for interpreting political action from the left in such a deep way.

Though I was aware of political happenings in the country in the early 1980s, I was not deeply involved in secondary school politics. When I completed secondary school, we were simply streamed to attend the UWC; there were literally no other choices. But it turned out well for me, and I am grateful. My family supported my further studies in many different ways.

JA: In some of your writings you talk about the notion of cultural justice, of having to live with the constant burden of self-consciousness, which is the result of having to function in a life world in which the dominant norms and codes are not those of your own social group. I'm wondering, how are practices of cultural injustice manifest on university campuses in South Africa today? Is the dual medium language policy [all courses are taught in both English

There is nobody innocent here 105

and Afrikaans] at the UFS an example of cultural injustice in relation to black students [Afrikaner students have the option of being taught in their mother tongue, while black students typically do not]?

How should cultural injustices be addressed on university campuses? I'm thinking of epistemic injustices, cultural injustices, this notion of having to function in an environment which is not your own. How do you understand this notion of cultural justice within the context of universities but specifically here at the UFS?

AK: Cultural injustice is probably the norm in most universities more than the exception. In fact, it is not necessarily a negative concept. It tries to frame, more or less, the reality of different kinds of people coming together in different kinds of spaces. At one time your codes will be missing; at another time your codes will be dominant. In five minutes' time, going into this office, going into another space, that can happen. You move from the presence of dominant codes that favor you into its absence in five or 10 minutes across these different kinds of spaces.

Cultural injustice happens when one has to give up one's taken-for-granted ways of being in the world. If a social context does not require this, one is obviously favored. This is difficult to accept, especially when the institutional culture fits with one's taken-for-granted assumptions, which results in preferential treatment. Being aware of this is important because it is from this position of consciousness that one can challenge injustices.

But at a very mundane everyday level, it is the student that is coming in here [to the UFS] with different codes and the way in which the two mix together. What kinds of communication will be legitimate, will be emerging out of that? It's like an ontological condition of human beings. The reason that particular consciousness is important is that, at the time of the communicative act, you are already sensitive to and reflect on what codes are present and absent and so on.

Critical self-consciousness has to do with a sense of being able to determine that. Then you know that you have to co-carry the burden of the absence of those particular codes and that you have to lower your privilege of having your codes present. Then you move into the space of cultural justice in the interaction between groups and individuals in those kinds of spaces.

One must be permanently and perpetually aware of the mechanisms by which these different injustices function and allow oneself to assist in the distribution of the burdens that come with the distribution of the different codes. My work on that has to do with political consciousness, with how codes are imported into a communicative space – how one is favored or disadvantaged by it and how one then manages those spaces. That's a permanent condition of communication.

One experiences cultural injustices at the university on a daily basis, but they can be educative moments that sharpen one's thinking and praxis of critical self-consciousness that can work against one's predisposition to be culturally arrogant.

106 *André Keet*

JA: So cultural justice requires sharing the burden of self-consciousness, of having a space where you meet, where you give up the desire to act only within your own dominant codes and reach out, by some sort of agreement or way of coming together, so that neither set of codes and practices dominate a communicative situation.

AK: It's precisely because of that where the notion of mutual vulnerability comes from. That's more or less the route that explains how mutual vulnerability can be intelligible and political.

JA: Yes, it leads right to your notion of mutual vulnerability. That is, I guess, the space in which you meet. Of course, there's always lots of code switching going on, especially where there are so many different cultural and ethnic groups, languages, etc. But I'm wondering, how do you see the dual medium language policy here at UFS? Does it perpetuate cultural injustice within the context of this university?

AK: For me, it's a very complex matter. I think that pragmatically, you will have to argue this thing very carefully. There are language rights, educational rights, and cultural rights in our constitution. Of course, we don't provide that [instruction in their mother tongue] for our black English instruction. On balance, I would argue that the dual language policy favors Afrikaans-speaking students. It is a form of cultural injustice because, pragmatically speaking, one cannot provide, at this moment, instruction in official black languages, which is also very expensive.

That's the big challenge. Do you then just create a medium, a language of instruction, that will take away the advantage [White Afrikaans-speaking students are typically proficient in English as well but overwhelmingly choose to take classes in their mother tongue. This academic advantage, and the resulting self-segregation of most Afrikaner students, would disappear if English became the lingua franca of instruction.]? If you value diversity in different kinds of ways, then you will have to make provision for Afrikaans-speaking students coming into the university spaces as well. The historical moment demands courageous decisions and practices, flexible and experimental spaces.

For instance, it will be sad for me if my child can go to a university where there are no white kids because that's part of the making of a new South Africa. I'm highly in favor of these kinds of diversities – in maintaining the presence of white students on our campus. According to demographic norms that one can employ, I think that's good for a university in general. I think that the challenges we face, that come with it, is an educational act. Not having them, you lose out; you don't gain. You lose out by not having those kinds of challenges present in the educational space. If you then, for pragmatic reasons, have to have a language policy that makes that possible, then you will have to argue: On what side do you win the most? Or the better question might be: On what side do you lose the least? Given the demographics of our university, this way forward should be obvious.

There is nobody innocent here   107

But the one thing that I know, which would be a step that I would support, is that you must keep the debate perpetually open. There must not be a firm position; the options will emerge if you keep the debate open. I would, for instance, think that having, say, a weekly or monthly seminar from various people only on the issue of the language question in South Africa will be a useful thing in its own right. You see, in time, the various options emerge. The idea of those kinds of seminars would be to bring forth the importance of language in meaning making in the world for all groups so that you don't think it's only your particular language, say for instance, Afrikaans, that is so important for meaning making.

There are 11 [official languages], and 27 other languages and language groups that can have the same kinds of terms. Then, of course, for us it would be better to get an understanding of the importance of language across the board for everybody. In different kinds of ways that particular discussion, hopefully, would throw up different kinds of options. You see, if we don't have the discussion, you will not get to a point where it will be OK for Afrikaans-speaking communities to come to an English instruction institution. For me, the step must be: Let's begin the debate so that in a year or two or three, it may be possible for Afrikaans communities to make that decision themselves. Of course, then for black students to have a space to express their discomfort. It's very difficult. There's a politics and a pragmatics that has to play, a pragmatism and a politics.

JA: This notion of deliberation is very central to your work. You claim that the exercise of values, as the exercise of legal claims, leads to conflict and a weakening of social solidarity, that disrespect and intolerance are related to the exercise of rights as legal claims. In your view, this represents an abdication of values to law, of the responsibility to reflect and to make moral judgments to law. It's this displacement of values to law.

In your writings about human rights as a set of legal rights, you argue that it can lead to conflict, that values and ethical principles get usurped into what you call the "human rights idol", that society terminates any substantive and critical public deliberation on these matters. Juridical forms of rights and values, without deliberative democracy, you argue, leads to social conflict.

You also argue that human rights idolatry has been unable to root a human rights value framework within the lived social realities and experiences of most people across the globe and that the creation of legal subjectivity can be deconstructed to reveal subjects who have rights but who lack equality and well-being. To remedy this situation, you argue that constitutional rights should reenter the life world, using Habermas's language, and be rooted within a normative, not a legal, validity. In other words, there's this notion that you can't just push off ethical questions and make them legal questions or make them into abstracted substantive rights. As you were talking about before, the norms have to be generated within the life world itself rather than imposed on it through a set of rights or legal claims. I can see that that's your

108   *André Keet*

approach to the language question as well. How does this view inform your understanding and practice of transformative citizenship?

AK: As an act of support for human rights, a rights critique has become central to my praxis since completing my PhD. I am very wary of the obsession to formulate human relations in legal terms. I am particularly attracted to the idea of rights reentering the life world, to be reanimated in our daily struggles and return to normative bases.

From African moral philosophy we learn that rights are framed in the language of contention, conflict, and self-regard. Therefore, I do not build my practice of transformative citizenship on rights idolatry but on rights critiques for two reasons. First, human rights are important, and secondly, they can have a deadening effect on citizenship and thus needs its internal critique to be productive for social justice work. Rights critiques can be industrious in setting human rights outside because they do not have as their starting point and center dominant discourses. I am thus less interested in focusing on political leaders as the epicenter of politics than working with the political in collaboration with my students.

In the South African context, there are many international examples of how rights fuel social conflicts because rights have to be claimed. The kinds of cases that we deal with here as well affirms that if you build a transitional democracy on a bridge of rights without attention given to how it is normatively justified, in fact, the rights language becomes the language of conflict. In fact, it's justified in that language as well. But of course, I don't give up on the [human rights] discourse because I think it's very important. I actually think it needs to be professionalized, only doing so by its critique, which is why it's one of my intellectual projects.

The challenge, for me then, would be if you look at educational research. I'll give you a very simple challenge. You look at educational research in South Africa post-1994 and especially research in the area of social justice. It kicks off from the conception of the rights in the constitution as if it provides a theoretical justification for the work that the author is trying to do. Just think of that; that is the easy work. Authors will kick off, and you can find it all over the place. If, for instance, they speak about equality, they say the South African Constitution, in section whatever, but since 1994 ABC has not happened. Then they go and explain the gap between policy and implementation, between the dream and the reality.

But just think where that researchable question is coming from. That researchable question comes from an idea that instead of being theorized is taken from the constitution as a provision without the necessary educational theorization that has gone into it. For instance, if you write about equality and education, don't come here and tell me that we require equality in education because the Universal Declaration of Human Rights and all those kinds of things say that nondiscrimination is important. Then they give you a whole page on the different kinds of international declarations and so on. But actually, you should argue: Why is equality a substantive value for the

There is nobody innocent here 109

actor, for education itself? Why would equality be important even if these things didn't exist, even if we didn't have a constitution?

The argument that they make is that equality is now important because we have a constitution that says so. It undercuts the quality of our research because it doesn't tell us how equality should be normatively grounded in education. It abdicates the responsibility for political thinking to the human rights framework. Instead of having the responsibility to think, we take that provision as law. Ethics is displaced into a [human rights] framework. What the rights do is that you have two contested claims, but deliberation is required to get to a balance between them.

Of course, if you then bring it back to the idea of how it influences the reading of transformative leadership, you see part of the reason why I work on particular outsides. I think interest in the state as politics is very limited. I actually do not want to spend lots of my time on that because I want to build the political outside leaders. All the political outsides are more or less my attempt, where the normative legitimacies are rooted in those kinds of interactions, so that when you invoke the right to equality, you don't evoke the right to equality because it's a right in the constitution. You invoke the right to equality because it has normative legitimacy in the way in which we act out our lives as human beings within the space of political outsiders.

Of course, it can sometimes get very complicated in those kinds of arguments. But for me, it would be that if you have a total awareness of the state as politics, you also abdicate agency. My task as a leader in this space, in working with youngsters, is that I am trying to shift that gaze; I want my students to look in a different direction. The reason I call them political outsiders is because they are political, but they're outside of this normal frame. That's what I hopefully achieve from time to time.

JA: Yeah, it's the same idea, looking to political leaders demobilizes democratic deliberation and all the rest. There's a notion of shifting responsibility, of abdicating one's own responsibility to make ethical choices or whatever. Initially, the institute's conceptual framework was Shared Complicities and Mutual Vulnerabilities: Democracies of Proximity and the Futures of Justice. Later on, you refined that a bit. How is the notion of shared complicities related to mutual vulnerabilities, and how do they inform your understanding of transformative citizenship?

AK: I wanted to develop a conceptual schema that reflects our history and present as messy, as a basis for thinking about collective futures. I am worried about the lazy historical thinking where victims, perpetrators, bystanders, and beneficiaries are neatly packaged and then imported into the present. An inclusive narrative of progress cannot emerge from these forms of thinking. This is not only incorrect but also risky as a form of praxis in transitional spaces.

I have witnessed firsthand the contributions of whites and blacks to the liberation struggle as a part of the antiapartheid movement and lived through a period when collaborators and supporters of the apartheid regime came across the racial divides: whites, blacks, coloreds, and Indians. This is the messiness of history that motivated me to look at shared complicities and mutual vulnerabilities as organizing themes of my work; the links between the two are conceptual and practical.

In South Africa what we have peddled post-94, and I suppose in many other countries such as Germany, the United States, and Israel, very sanitized versions of history so that you can identify victims and perpetrators, bystanders and beneficiaries. You can have a repackaging of those because it makes the demands that one can make in the present more intelligible. That is a lazy way of thinking. It's also a lazy way of working through politics in a transitional space.

History has society captured in a web of complicities. The identification of victims and perpetrators is not so easy; some may be victims one day and perpetrators the day after. Our history is replete with those. On the one hand, you have white South Africans who participated in the cultural uprising against their parents in the 80s. There was the end conscription campaign; there were many things like that. I joined the UDF, which was more or less set up by Afrikaner students from Stellenbosch University. For me, history can't be so clear-cut. Then, during that same period, you have blacks voting for the Bantustan governments with high participation rates, participating in the apartheid structure via a legal act. Then you have the coloreds and the Indians voting in the bicameral parliament in another apartheid structure.

If you look at history like that, then your categories of perpetrator and so on collapse. Then the only concept that makes sense is shared complicities. 'Shared complicities' is a term that wants to make history as messy as it was and, on that basis, develop better ways for dealing with the present. You see, if you can have white students understand that there were a sizable number of whites who fought the apartheid government, which is true, it will make their sense of the present much more valuable and productive. If you can get black students to understand that many of our communities participated in the apartheid regime, it will make their sense of the present also a bit more open and hospitable to different kinds of groups that we're coming from. The only thing left, in any case, after history has made its mark, is complicity.

Coming to a university, there is nobody innocent here. That's why I'm interested in what people would call negative concepts. But I actually don't see them as negative: complicity and guilt. Then, of course, you get to the complexities once you have sorted out those. I work from the perspective of making myself and other people understand that we are in a space where the right to be guilty is *more* important than your drive to be innocent. In fact, both guilt and complicity are more agential concepts than innocence. Innocence terminates your responsibility and your agency: Guilt demands it; complicity demands it. We know that apartheid is evil; that's a given. But the way in which it played itself out, the social realities, are a bit more complex than we would like them to be.

Significance and implications

As previously stated, Professor Keet's intellectual project focuses on creating the conditions in which new normative values and practices can emerge within inclusive, democratic, and deliberative contexts. In institutions of higher education, this means grounding norms and practices in the subjective experience and ontological orientations of students. It also means creating culturally just learning environments characterized by "a totally new set of vulnerabilities" in which no group's cultural codes are privileged (Keet, Zinn, & Porteus, 2009, p. 115).

Professor Keet is deeply concerned with the workings of power, with how it functions in communicative spaces, disciplines, and institutional structures, and with the relation between discourses and the formation of subjectivity. In seeking to transform normative values, practices, concepts, and subjectivities, whether in education, human rights discourse, or conceptions of leadership, one of Professor Keet's primary aims is to activate agency and citizenship, to incite individuals to grapple with ethical choices rather than abdicate their responsibility to politics or law. He theorizes the educational dimension of transformation through concepts such as shared complicities, mutual vulnerability, and academic citizenship, which make it possible to think differently about the past and the present and to imagine possible futures.

Reference

Keet, A., Zinn, D., & Porteus, K. (2009). Mutual vulnerability: A key principle in a humanizing pedagogy in post-conflict societies. *Perspectives in Education*, 27(2), 109–119.

7 Transformation as an intellectual and ethical project

Changing inherited patterns of thought and social practice

Lis Lange

Dr. Lis Lange is the acting vice rector (academic) of the University of the Free State (UFS) and senior director of the Directorate for Institutional Research and Academic Planning (DIRAP). Prior to arriving at the UFS in 2011, Dr. Lange was the executive director of the Higher Education Quality Committee of the Council for Higher Education, which is responsible for quality assurance of private and public institutions of higher education, and the acting CEO of the Council on Higher Education, which advises the minister of higher education.

Dr. Lange was involved in the development and implementation of science and technology in higher education in South Africa through the Human Sciences Research Council, the National Research Foundation, and the Council on Higher Education. She was a board member of the International Network of Quality Assurance Agencies in Higher Education, an editor of *Acta Academica*, a journal that focuses on the humanities, and a board member and reviewer for a number of other South African journals of higher education.

Dr. Lange was born and grew up in Argentina and attended the University of Buenos Aires during the military dictatorship (1976–1983), where she received a BA honors in history. She went on to earn an MA in African studies from the *El Colegio de Mexico* and a PhD in history from the University of Witwatersrand in 1998. Her doctoral dissertation examines the emergence of the white working class in South Africa from 1890 to 1922.

Dr. Lange is also a public intellectual who, in addition to producing scholarly research and policy reports, has written articles about educational policy for national publications such as the *Mail & Guardian*. She has taught at universities in Argentina and South Africa and delivered keynote addresses at professional conferences and institutions of higher education.

In contemporary South Africa, discourse about transformation in higher education typically focuses on performance-orientated, quantifiable metrics in relation to the racial demographics of the nation. This particular understanding of transformation became hegemonic, Dr. Lange argues, because the conceptualization of transformation in the early 1990s was "oversimplified" by global discourses of efficiency and the logic of the market and was reduced "to numbers, percentages, and ratios" and thus to equity (Lange, 2010, 2013).

Transformation as an intellectual   113

In her view, this simplified notion of transformation depoliticizes knowledge and perpetuates inherited patterns of thinking, social practices, and "established knowledge" of the other. When transformation is "frozen in numbers," Dr. Lange argues, three forms of knowledge that are crucial to transformation, "knowledge of the self, knowledge of knowledge (knowledge of the epistemological foundations of the disciplines) and knowledge of the other" are eclipsed in national discourse about transformation. While significantly increasing educational opportunity for previously marginalized and excluded groups is an important goal, she argues that these types of knowledge, and the values and ethical commitments that academics bring to their work, are essential to transforming institutions of higher education in South Africa.

Dr. Lange argues that good leadership requires good citizenship, that leaders must also be "republican citizens" who cultivate people's capacity for agency and public deliberation. For educational leaders, this means providing students with opportunities to practice judgment by "developing pedagogies that enlarge their capacity to imagine other worlds and other people's suffering" and helping them "realize and experience that understanding is both an intellectual and a moral operation" that "must be opened to doubt and scrutiny" (Lange, July 29, 2012).

Dr. Lange has a strong ethical commitment to open and honest dialogue, unconstrained self-examination and critique, and the pursuit of personal and historical truth. In capitalist societies, which by definition are unequal and unjust, she argues that leaders must acknowledge that their participation in the public dialogue about transformation is made possible by the labor of others, and that this entails an ethical obligation to seek truth and promote the common good.

Dr. Lange (hereafter **LL**) began our conversation by talking about how she conceptualizes leadership for transformation and social justice.

LL: I locate my understanding of leadership very specifically within higher education and what I do. It has to do with the manner in which I, and a whole lot of other people with whom I've been working for the last 20 years, understand the notion of transformation.

For me, leadership for social justice or leadership for transformation is the kind of leadership that understands that social justice or transformation are not something which is superimposed; it's not something that you add on to what you do: It is something that you do *in* what you do. It has to come from inside, and it has to shape your conceptualizations and your practices, whatever your practices are, whether it's teaching and learning, the way in which you manage staff, your institutional culture. But for me, leadership for social justice or transformation is one that realizes transformation in the very *act* of being and doing things. I've been fighting for that thing for a long time.

JA: So you transform the university by being transformative in your own work, in your own life.

LL: I think that everybody who understands things in this way struggles because the target is mobile; it changes. Any sort of cast-in-stone definition of

114   *Lis Lange*

transformation is silly because transformation today is not what it was in 1994 or what is was in 1980. In 1980 we're not talking about transformation; it was a relatively new term. I mean the late 1980s, in any case.

You need to really find, and need to refine the conceptualization, and the target, and the methodology of implementation, and all these sort of things. In terms of characteristics of leadership, I would say that leadership under these circumstances has to be fundamentally critical and self-critical. I mean, you never arrive; you're always in the process of refinement and trying to get people to understand it. That's one of the main characteristics for me.

JA: Just to follow up on that, how does your understanding of leadership for social justice inform your conception and practice of leadership at the UFS?

LL: I must confess that of all the things that people are preoccupied with in higher education, I have never been particularly preoccupied with the definition of leadership or the practice of leadership – certainly in myself. Of all the things that I have read, probably the things in which I read the least are about leadership. But I do believe that one is all the time modeling what one wants the place to be; and different people have different styles in these things.

I tend to, not provoke, but I mean I tend to put the cards on the table. And I tend to point out areas which I think are problematic, and I do not try to make it pretty. When I interact with my own staff [in DIRAP], I believe that transformation is something that you do all the time. Let me give you an example. If we needed to do institutional research, the manner in which that research is constructed, the manner in which we conceptualize it, the manner in which we think we can use it, all of those things are part of the transformative process. Making the staff aware of what is the relationship between pass marks and social justice is part of the process of changing the manner in which people work. But I don't have a great theorization of leadership, I'm afraid.

JA: In many ways your approach to leadership reminds me of Professor Jansen's [Jonathan Jansen, the vice chancellor and rector of the UFS] recent speech at the Open Day assembly [an annual event for prospective students and their families in which he forcefully and unapologetically reiterated the core values and principles that undergird his vision of transformation at the UFS] is what comes to mind when I hear you talk about leadership, in terms of having a principled position, and that's all there is to it, of not trying to massage what you say.

LL: No, I don't think that that works. I think that one of the problems that one faces in these things is that – Jonathan probably does it very different from what I do – is how much one empathizes. I am not particularly empathic. I don't think I am, at least not if the benchmark is Jonathan. I am less patient. I'm still struggling to see what is the difficulty in understanding that every white individual in this country benefitted directly or indirectly from apartheid and why people should feel so resentful at the mere fact of this being pointed out to them. I find it difficult to understand.

Transformation as an intellectual 115

This does not mean that I expect everybody to carry a burden of guilt. But I think that from that point of departure, I benefitted, and will continue to benefit, because of my position in this society. For us [whites], there are a number of commitments, and you may or may not take them. For me, it is inevitable to take them. In that sense I think that Jonathan is more open to all the difficulties that people find to reconcile themselves to this notion. I'm trying to understand a bit better. I'm trying to understand how difficult it is for individuals who, for a number of reasons, do not have the elements to shift or do not have the elements to understand what the shift would look like; to be scared, to be reluctant, that I understand. But what I do not understand is their evasion of the moral moment; that I can't understand.

JA: I'm curious about what personal and professional experiences inform your understanding and practice of leadership. Were there major moments, experiences, or turning points in your life? Were there events or important people who influenced your development and thinking about leadership for transformation and social justice?

LL: Well, I've been all my life a very political being. Definitive moments in my life in terms of social justice and a conception of education as a political act. Well, I was born in Argentina, and I lived under the last military dictatorship [1976–1983], and I was fairly active in politics, as much as one could under the military dictatorship, but particularly towards the end of it. The whole movement of the Mothers of the *Plaza de Mayo* [an association of mothers whose children were disappeared by the military dictatorship that held demonstrations for many years in front of the presidential palace in Buenos Aires to find out what happened to their loved ones] and the whole calling for justice for missing people, for the *desaparecidos*, was an absolute turning point in my life. The Truth Commission in Argentina [the National Commission on the Disappeared, created in 1983 to investigate the disappearances] was a fundamental point in my political life and in my consciousness as a human being. When you come to South Africa, it was a very dangerous place before the elections. It's a society that can anesthetize you because it is so segregated that you may not see. If you don't see you may not feel, and you may not understand, and you may not imagine. It's a difficult place to negotiate.

The extraordinary moment for me was once when I just arrived in the country in 1990, and I was getting into a bus in a bus stop, and I was prevented from doing so by some other people traveling with me because it was a blacks-only bus; I found it extraordinary. I came here to do my doctorate, and when I finished my doctorate I started working in the funding branch of the Human Science Research Council, in the disbursing agency. There I met a bunch of people who had been involved in the struggle for many years and who had incredibly sharp minds and sharp moral compasses. I grew up with them, basically. I learned the dangers that one faces with one's own complacency: how being a white person carries a very peculiar burden of judgment that you do not realize even that you're making.

I had a fight, I suppose it was a fight, with one of my colleagues who was junior to me, while I was in this work. He was a young black man, and I thought that something that he had done was wrong or inappropriate. But evidently the manner in which I rendered this thing, and the manner in which I commented to some other colleagues to express my dissatisfaction with his work, made him accuse me of racism, and he was right. I did not realize what it was, why it was, and whatever. But I mean, a painful process of self-examination allowed me to realize that maybe he was right. The moment in which the 'maybe' was introduced, then I could see much more than otherwise I would have allowed myself to. These are the kinds of things you learn, to watch yourself, and then you become very sensitive to your own behavior. Sometimes I can see myself doing what I am doing. Which is not bad all the time because then you can see yourself this close to the abyss, to just putting your feet in the wrong place, and then you correct your course. Those things have been very important.

The other thing that was absolutely fundamental for me was when I changed jobs again and I started working with the Higher Education Quality Committee. Through that work I had the opportunity of visiting almost every single public higher education institution in the country and talk to students and staff, and to management – to feel the institutional culture, to feel the pain of some people, to feel the disarray and the irresponsibility. Then you think it's more complex: This is not a black and white problem only. You can see the complicated things; you see the students at one university beating each other up, to death, actually, because they belong to different political factions. You realize the extent of the damage. All those things, I cannot tell you one thing in particular, but all those things change you, make you see things differently.

JA: I saw that you did your master's degree in Mexico and then came to South Africa in the early 90s to get your doctorate. What drew you to South Africa after living through the military dictatorship in Argentina?

LL: Because of the similarities. I was very interested in the process of knowledge, truth, and power in the Foucauldian [the French philosopher Michel Foucault] manner that happened in Argentina. After doing my master's thesis in Mexico that was about the South African state, I was fascinated by the capacity of the South African state to create truth and power and the microphysics of power in the country. I wanted to see this thing up close quarters, and one of the things that I found most fascinating as a lefty was why it was possible that the white working class in this country was not following what one would imagine is orthodox class consciousness: That was what drew me here as a problem. But what also drew me here as a problem was the amazing quality of the historiographic production in this country. The discussion about the state in South Africa was theoretically extraordinarily interesting, and the historiography in this country was just competing easily with the best English and French social history, so I wanted to be here.

JA: What was your experience of the liberation struggle, and how did it inform your thinking?

LL: I did not have a direct experience of the liberation struggle in this country. I have a political experience in my own country, and those things mark you forever. I was a member of the Revolutionary Communist Party in Argentina; that's the Chinese Leninist party. Quite aside from the critique that one can do of Maoism and whatever, there were many aspects of the political education that we received that marks you forever in terms of the morals of the communists; in terms of the straightforwardness with which you work; in terms of the manner in which you treat people – you know, these kinds of things.

Then when I came here I was fortunate enough to meet a whole lot of people who were very involved in the struggle, and I learned from them. Then I've seen directly the things that can happen on the personal level. I have a daughter whom I have adopted. Her mother was killed in the last bits of the transition; she was an *Umkhonto we Sizwe* [Zulu for "Spear of the Nation," the armed wing of the ANC] soldier and was killed in a complicated situation in KZN [KwaZulu-Natal province]. You see the devastation that the struggle could cause at the individual levels, and then you empathize with individual pain and the toll that it takes.

I don't think that people think about those issues, actually. We have kind of forgotten the individuals and the scars that the struggle has left in many people, people who have been incarcerated, and have ended up alcoholics, or persecuted by the security police and their life destroyed. One can think of all those things only in political terms, but there are personal emotional terms for that.

JA: In one of your writings you talked about going to college under the dictatorship and that you would drive off, away from the cities, to have book groups where you would discuss books and ideas and politics. Was that experience part of this?

LL: That was not under the Communist Party; but yeah. This is one of the reasons why, for me, knowledge and the curriculum are such fundamental aspects of all of this. You see, when we were students in Argentina under the military dictatorship, both the teachers and the books were banned. There were certain things to which you did not have access. You could not read [Karl] Marx; you could not read [Henri] Lefebvre; you could not read [Ernest] Bloch. I mean you could hardly find a copy of [Ferdinand] Saussure; it was absurd. What we did was to read underground. We used to photocopy and infringe every aspect of copyright available, and that's what we did. Our resistance, our activism, was an intellectual activism because then we were in a position to critique the curriculum that we were being fed. This is what I'm trying to get the students to understand, that they have an active role to play in this institution; the curriculum does not belong to the university, it belongs to them too.

118   *Lis Lange*

Unfortunately, our students are in a difficult position in that regard because they have fewer tools than the ones that we had when I was at university. We were being educated in our own language; we had every single book available. Nationally we came, not all of us, from middle-class families because the University of Buenos Aires, being a free university, allowed for anybody to come in. One of my best friends, her parents were domestic workers; it's a different kind of environment. But still, we were all educated people in ways that our students are not; for them it's more difficult.

JA: That comes through in a lot of your writing, how the intellectual rigor of your own education, your own experience, is being lost in contemporary higher education. You talk about losing the intellectual depth and fullness and rigor of intellectual life and how that's related to the neoliberal transformation of universities internationally. You've already talked about your racial identity and how that affects your practice of leadership for social justice, but you've talked less about your gender identity. Does your gender identity inform your understanding and practice of leadership for transformation and social justice at the UFS? Is it something that's important?

LL: No, it's not. I say it almost shamefully because, you see, I came to politics through Marxism; I didn't come to politics from feminism. I grew up in a family in which, although my father was probably a very abrasive man as a husband, he was certainly an absolute and unbelievably enabling father of his only daughter. My father thought there were no limits to what I could and I should do and affirmed me constantly. My father thought that the stupidest thing that I could do was to get married and have children. But in Argentina there are very many powerful women at the university level; there were many women professors and higher [top management]. I never had the real experience of gender discrimination until I came to South Africa.

When I came to South Africa I started realizing that your gender is a very important thing. I had extraordinary experiences; one was here in the Free State. Many years ago I was working at the National Research Foundation [an independent government agency that promotes and supports research and rates the scholarship of academics in South Africa]. I was a sort of middle-level official. I came to an institution to do a presentation, or something like that, and they had invited me to a dinner or something. One of the male professors who I was interacting with, I had a doctorate by then, introduced me to his wife as, "Dear, this is Lis, the girl from the NRF." I mean I told him what I thought of the introduction, but I found it extraordinary.

You can see it here, at this university in particular, but it's not just this university; the level of patriarchy is just extraordinary. In all the task teams here that I participate in at a high level, 90% of the time I'm the only woman. All these slightly complicated technical things, like we're doing a viability model for academic departments, these old men and I. I joke about it and all that. I try to use a sense of humor a lot to drive these sort of messages home, but they don't always get there. Sometimes because the joke, if it is a bit too

Transformation as an intellectual   119

sharp or too subtle, goes over the heads of people that do not have a sense of humor. Other times, because of just sheer thick skin, they don't see it. But no, I'm afraid that gender has never been as important to me as race and as class and all these kinds of things in my own personal experience until the revelation happened here. But I'm not as strong, theoretically, in feminism in the way in which I read other things. I suppose it is a defect of my formation, my education, but there are so many things to do.

JA: You're less concerned with identity politics than class politics?

LL: Yea, identity politics is not my thing. I'm not even all that drawn to queer studies or any of those things. I mean if the students ask me to talk, as they have a couple of times, asked me about being gay or ideas of gayness . . . I mean I have read a fair amount about these things, and I can talk about it. But again, these are not the fundamental issues that define me or that make me feel definition of others.

JA: Do religious beliefs inform your understanding and practice of leadership?

LL: Look, they say that once a Catholic, always a Catholic. I was born a Catholic. I was educated in a Catholic school, in a convent school, for 12 years in Buenos Aires. I was very drawn, and very actively drawn, to the liberation theology movement in Latin America. I read and used and argued every piece of Catholic church document with which one could define redistribution, socialism, etc., as something that was the way in which the world should be ordained according to God.

God and I fought when the Church in Argentina, almost en masse, supported the military dictatorship. When I opted to be in the Communist Party, a priest almost threatened me with excommunication. I fought with the Church when the first time I had sex with a boyfriend, you know, and these kind of things. Over the years the sense of power, and dirt, and accommodation, and self-serving things – threats – threw me completely away from Church and these kinds of things. I think that I was very critical, particularly of the Dutch Reform Church under apartheid, and sometimes I still find it very difficult to deal with that. I suppose, yes, religious beliefs might have formed part of how I grew up, how I saw the world. Now there is no God, but I mean the vision is the same. But I believe in a spirituality; I believe that it is important to have a kind of center. It's a strange combination of religion, Buddhism, psychoanalysis, and Marxism.

As a good Argentinian, I have many years of psychoanalysis and Lacanian [the French psychoanalyst and philosopher Jacques Lacan] psychoanalysis at that. I think psychoanalysis gives you an amazing instrument to think, and if you don't want to be naïve about yourself, psychoanalysis and Lacanian psychoanalysis can be your friend. Of course, it can be a fantastic sort of excuse to escape in very important words and metaphors. But I think that for anybody who has a concern about truth, the experience of psychoanalysis is very important. I'm always more interested in knowing the truth and not in feeling OK. I don't care about being sad or depressed: I just want to know why. I'd rather feel crappy than deluded!

120   *Lis Lange*

JA: It's clear that your understanding of leadership for social justice informs your practice, but what does it look like?

LL: I think you should ask that to the people who see it; I do not know. I think it is fundamentally argumentative. I mean this is a university, and as such, I suppose, ideally at least, it should be built on intellectual argument. For me, it's about making things explicit. For me, it's not enough to have a guideline as to how to produce a good program. For me, it is important to develop the framework that situates the curriculum within the broader spectrum of these things, and this is what I do. Everything that I do starts with a kind of framework that lays out the thing and tries to explain how these things that we are doing in this particular corner of the university build towards the broader issues that Jonathan [Jansen] has put in place here.

For me, it's a continuation of a conversation that started many years ago. I mean this is a particular incarnation, if you want, a manifestation of that conversation. But it was no different when we were working on quality assurance at the system level. I can see now, sometimes, when I look at things that I have written in the past, how the same themes obsessively come back and repeat themselves, and new experiences, and new readings, and new conversations make the conceptualization sharper and more sophisticated.

I think that the other thing I am always concerned about is the normative aspect. For me, there is a fundamental issue about how the good society and the good life go together. There is an element of personal passion and commitment in this that I try and put across. I think that this is one of the reasons why I'm so interested in the work of Hannah Arendt because Arendt was concerned about judgment and how judgment and politics and these kinds of things go together.

JA: What then is the relationship between knowledge and ethics? How does your understanding of that relationship inform your practice at the UFS?

LL: You see, I believe that the manner in which we teach and the things that we teach should enable our students to make moral judgments. This has to do with the kind of questions that they ask. I tried to write a paper about this, and I was taking several examples (Lange, July 29, 2012). One of the examples that I took was how one can understand and analyze the financial crisis. If you look at the financial crisis, and you said this was due to the greed of some people, the response is to tell the greedy people: Don't do this again. But there is another way of analyzing this thing, and it is to see whether it's a systemic issue that allows for this thing to happen. The critique should not be of the person but should be of the system.

I think that is both a knowledge proposition and an ethical question for which you need to decide; you need to decide what it is that you want to do. What is your position in relation to the possibilities opened by the research on the human genome? That's also important; these are the kinds of things. I think that what Helga Nowotny [professor emeritus of social studies of science at UTH Zurich, the Swiss Federal Institute of Technology in Zurich,

Transformation as an intellectual 121

Austria] calls socially robust knowledge is problematic in the sense that she thinks it has to be a sort of consensual agreement as to what is important in relation to the thing. But she doesn't give the step of saying sometimes these things also have an ethical dimension; we need to consider this ethical dimension. Anyway, I struggle with those things.

JA: I would like to return to a question I raised earlier. Could you talk a little more about the personal and institutional challenges you face here at the UFS?

LL: The greatest personal challenge is to try and find empathy: I'm trying. I think that I'm a bit better now than when I came but just marginally. I find it difficult not to label some of the practices that I see as mediocrity and use the label in my conversations with people. I'm starting to learn to think that if people do not have the elements to deal with this thing for a number of reasons, maybe a more compassionate and empathetic approach would be better than this confrontational thing. Maybe I need to find people who understand what I'm saying but at the same time can interpret it for other people better than I can say it. I'm at that stage of my evolution here.

At the personal level, I think that often I come across very harsh, harsher than I actually am, as if the only thing that I am is harsh. I am very harsh; I am very harsh with myself before anything else. But I think that in relation to people, I'm learning to moderate that, certainly with my staff, the people I work with directly; it is easier because we get to know each other. I have learned over the years how to provide a critique about things that is enabling instead of being so tough. This is also tough; it is not easy. But that's at the personal level.

Institutionally, what I found the most difficult to deal with is passive resistance and passive aggression, for which there is plenty. It is usually accompanied by a lack of truth, inauthentic behavior, so people never tell you what they actually think, which drives me crazy. Those are the most difficult things for me. I mean I'd rather hear, "You are impossible; you are arrogant; we don't want to do this; we think that what you're talking about is crap." But they don't tell you that. They smile at you, offer meek resistance, if at all, or they tell you yes, and they do very little. Or if they seem to be doing something, the something that they do returns back, not in all cases, the same thing that you were trying to change. This is the thing that I do not like.

Of course, in the middle of all of this there is exactly the opposite, there are the people who actually want to do it and who are working for change and all that, but you asked me what were the most difficult things. The passive resistance, particularly, because for somebody who's obsessed about truth your impulse is to try and uncover it, but it strategically doesn't work. You need to work around it; you need to undermine it from below in a sense. It's very demanding for somebody with a personality like mine. But it's nice; it's fun at very many moments.

122 *Lis Lange*

JA: You try to work around resistance rather than confront it directly?

LL: Not all the time – sometimes I do. This is the funny thing, you see. It is easier to confront these things in the big ideas. It is easy for me at the meeting to say this thing about how white people benefitted from apartheid to the horror or otherwise of everybody else. But what is more difficult is to take this curriculum and to say, "In this curriculum these are the moments in which you are reproducing the system." That's because this is the moment in which there is incomprehension. The big idea is not so difficult; it is the fine work that is the difficult one. You can make speeches, that's fine, and people may or may not take your speeches.

The thing that is the most difficult is that some people think that what they teach is neutral, and they believe that because they say it is neutral; it is not political. They do not understand that neutrality isn't neutral but that it's profoundly political. It's two languages and two conceptions of the world clashing. What I propose is political; what they do is not political. It's the way in which knowledge is constructed; this is the way we always have done it: That is hard.

JA: Well, it's clear that you encounter resistance to your leadership.

LL: Yes, I'm very good at provoking it all by myself!

JA: Is your response to resistance informed by your understanding of leadership?

LL: As I said, I don't think a hell of a lot about leadership. I think a lot about change and strategies for change. I tend to think a lot and analyze a lot things that happened, and how they have been happening, and where we have gone wrong in certain things. For me, one of the issues that I'm working on now is how, in the process of policy making in the country in general, and at different universities in particular, we have not done anything to include academics in this process of change. The government has included the top echelons of the institutions, and people have paid attention to students as a new sort of stakeholder sector, but the academics are squashed between the management and the students.

For me, what I'm trying to do right now is to try and ask the questions that I think that only academics can answer. The work that I do in institutional research is: What is it that you want to know? What are the questions that I'm not asking you that you want me to ask you? I think that this is opening up the possibility of a conversation. It's still not happening, but I think that we're opening that possibility, and I think that's important. We cannot change this thing unless we change it together with the academics. We have absolutely no control. I mean, the university is what happens in the environment of the classroom, the curriculum, the laboratory, the group, the tutorials – you name it – and all the other things. But it's fundamentally this.

We have absolutely no control over that, and it's great that we don't have control. But then we need to gain the trust of the people who have control over that, to a point. Then we need to hear what they have to say, what the problems are, the things that they find difficult. Why is it that they do not understand? Why do they think we are insane sometimes with what we say?

Transformation as an intellectual 123

I'm trying to listen to what people have to say and see whether we can find a way of working together. But as I said, it's just the very beginning of this; I don't know what's going to happen.

JA: Given what you just talked about, what keeps you going in the face of resistance to your leadership? What are the things in the daily struggle of transformation, in trying to make fundamental changes to university practices, to university life, that keep you going?

LL: I think on the one hand there's a community of practice, an expression which I hate, but it is an elegant way of talking about one's comrades. The people who talk the same language, the people who challenge you, the people who push you further, that makes me want to do this. Then there's small realizations, small moments in which the thing happens; then you want to keep on going. When something that you perceived, almost intuitively, is confirmed through hard-nosed research, you feel affirmed, and then you want to continue because if the diagnosis is correct, then maybe the medicine is also correct.

Then there are the events that move you at the personal level. You know, a little bout of racism, and you see the pain around this place and say, "Well, this thing needs changing; we need to change it," like the appalling behavior of the convocation [an assembly of primarily Afrikaner alumni] of this university a week ago [where Reverend Rudi Buys, the former Dean of Student Affairs, was vilified]. These are the kinds of things that keep me going because I cannot believe that there are people in the world that think like that.

The other day the Minister of Home Affairs Naledi Pandor was here. She was minister of education when I was in the Council on Higher Education. She came for election purposes. She gave a fantastic account of the things that this country has achieved in 20 years of higher education, and science and technology, which are the two portfolios that she managed before this current one. I was thinking to myself, "You know, we've done so much; we have achieved so much, and yet there is so much that still needs to be done." It's that kind of thing.

On optimistic days I think we do make a difference. I think that every student who turns around to ask you for another lecture is a difference that you made – every time that you bump into somebody that says you changed my life. I don't think that I have ever changed anybody's life, but people tell you these sorts of things and you say, "Wow, that's great."

Changing systems is very difficult, and changing institutions is very difficult. I think that we have achieved some things; they are small things, and nobody will have noticed these building blocks. People will take everything for granted, but in the end it will help change things. You change practices slowly, and then practices change practices. It takes a long time; it takes longer than one term as vice chancellor: It's a very long thing. There has to be continuity for these changes to actually take root. That's the reason why

124   *Lis Lange*

I'm so glad that Jonathan has continued the work we need to do [Jonathan Jansen was reappointed for a second five-year term as vice chancellor and rector in 2014].

JA: You argue that transformation has been reduced to numbers at institutions of higher education and that the ethical dimension has been lost. Could you elaborate a bit? What does transformation mean to you, and how does your understanding of transformation inform your practice of leadership for social justice?

LL: I've been struggling with this thing of transformation for a long time. Recently, I wrote something about it (Lange, September 6, 2013). I think that transformation has to do with the building of a society that undoes apartheid and puts something in place that is its opposite, that negates it in practice. I think this has different manifestations in different areas.

In higher education, for me, there is a way of analyzing this thing. It has a lot to do with knowledge again. I think that there are three types of knowledge that one needs to master to try and manage transformation, which are knowledge of knowledge, of the curriculum, of the research that you do – these kind of things. Then it's the knowledge of the institution itself, which has to do with the manner in which the institutional culture, history, and these things get in the way of a different society. This is not just about historically white institutions, or historically English institutions; it's about everybody. We all have our own little things to think about and correct.

Then there is knowledge of the other, and the other is a broad other; it is the other that is a colleague who does not look like me or does not speak my language; the other is the students; the other is the community; the other is a whole lot of others that come into higher education. I think that the dialectic between these things is where transformation happens, that what institutions need to do is to generate knowledge of what is happening in these three domains.

I think my office tries to do that for this institution. Of course, this inevitably permeates the manner in which I understand leadership; and the manner in which I talk to my staff; and the manner in which I talk to colleagues in the faculties; and the manner in which I interact with the [university] senate. I'm trying to make people aware of the importance of these types of knowledge and of the necessity of making them conscious because they are there; they are operating in a subterranean kind of way.

In the latest version of this knowledge of transformation, we just sent it off to a journal, I talk about the difference between the knowledge that emerges out of Catholic confession and the knowledge that emerges within a psychoanalytical process. I'm more interested in psychoanalytical processing because, you see, I'm not interested in absolution; I'm interested in getting a change, and absolution doesn't necessarily bring change.

We have general staff meetings in the directorate every six weeks; the meeting has two parts. Everybody meets, from the secretary to the highest person, administrative persons, everybody. The first part of the meeting usually has a reading. The week before I send out one or two readings; they may be policies, they may be research that we ourselves have produced, and therefore everybody needs to be familiar with it and understand the consequences that it has. In one of these rounds I gave them this paper about the knowledges of transformation. I gave them that, and I gave them the paper that I wrote about curriculum here at the university not because I'm interested in people knowing about what I write but because I thought that it was the most condensed way of putting on the table a conceptualization of something that for me was important for the manner in which we work.

I tried to explain to them why the role of every single person that works in this directorate is important because all of us, one way or the other, are sustaining this thing. From the person who books the flights of a reviewing panel, to the ones that are controlling the quality of the modules in a program, to the ones who are number crunching to see where we are with the environments, to the ones that do the sort of sexier research about the student perceptions of whatever. For me, they need to be, and they need to feel part of, a change project – the meaning that the work has. People come to work because they need to earn money; they have a job. For some people, maybe, it's just that. But in general I think that for some people it is something that has meaning. For me, that's important.

JA: Is there anything we have not discussed that you would like to talk about?

LL: I suppose there is one issue when one discusses these things. It feels as if one has a complete, close-on focus on the institution, or on the individual, or whatever. I really believe that transformation and social justice are much bigger things than higher education. You need to have an economic model that allows for social justice. We operate [in higher education] within the limits of a structural situation, and I think that it is important to remind oneself of that thing. Higher education is a minimum corner in the bigger scheme of things in terms of social justice in this country. It's a very privileged lot, and a very small one. For me, it is always very important to make sure that we understand our size in relation to a bigger problem.

JA: The limits of what is politically possible?

LL: Yeah, absolutely. We cannot change society through or in higher education; we can critique, but we cannot change society. We are very much constrained by the absolute limits of the political model, the financial model, the economic model, and the social relations of this country – the ones that are still not transformed. That's the only thing, I think.

JA: Given that, what is the function and role of higher education in terms of its relationship to larger developmental issues, to political issues?

LL: I think it is clear by now that higher education has a very important role to play from a developmental point of view if you think of all the professions and all the areas of the life of a society that higher education takes care of, so of speak. But I also think that we are very often falling in the trap of believing that if we produce the skills, then the labor market will absorb all the skills, and then we will all be happy. This is not the world in which the capitalist system works. One of the fundamental premises of the capitalist system is that there have to be people who do not have work. We have this obsessive skills discourse and skills drive, which is fine to a point. But then we all buy uncritically into the knowledge economy, and the innovation economy, and the innovation society, and you name it. All of those things are true, but at the same time there's a critical edge to that one needs to keep an eye on. Because if not, we're just sort of fantasizing and not realizing that there is always a level of exploitation that it is happening for us to do what we are doing: Who pays for it? These are the kinds of things I think higher education should be doing more, which is doing its critical role, which we don't do very much. We are a very quiet system; there's not a hell of a lot of critique in these areas.

Significance and implications

Dr. Lange's life and work are marked by a relentless pursuit of truth in self-understanding, interpersonal relations, and disciplinary knowledge. She argues that educational leaders should be republican citizens who cultivate agency and public deliberation and provide students with opportunities to critique the discourses, forms of disciplinary knowledge, and curricula disseminated by the university. In her view, students have the right and responsibility to examine the moral foundations of knowledge and to demand alternative epistemologies.

Dr. Lange seeks to interrupt inherited patterns of thought and practice that maintain forms of privilege and limit what can be thought and the kinds of subjectivity that are possible. She wants to democratize the notion of leadership and argues that universities should educate citizens and develop citizen-leaders who are responsive to communities. Dr. Lange wants students and others to understand that forms of disciplinary knowledge and pedagogical practices are imbued with moral choices and that these choices can be excavated, challenged, and displaced.

References

Lange, L. (May 21, 2010). The trouble with transformation. *Mail & Guardian*. Retrieved from http://mg.co.za/article/2010–05–21-the-trouble-with-transformation

Lange, L. (July 29, 2012). Leadership qualities require good citizenship. *The Sunday Independent*.

Lange, L. (2012). Understanding and action: Thinking with Arendt about democratic education. *Perspectives in Education*, 30(4), 1–8.

Lange, L. (September 6, 2013). Transformation by numbers skims the surface of tertiary realities. *Mail & Guardian*. Retrieved from http://mg.co.za/article/2013–09–06-transformation-by-numbers-skims-the-surface-of-tertiary-realities

8 A new hope
Believing in a fairer, more decent, and more humane society

John Samuel

Mr. John Samuel has been a tireless warrior for social justice for more than 50 years. He is one of South Africa's most distinguished and internationally recognized education experts and leaders. Mr. Samuel grew up in a small rural village on the north coast of KwaZulu-Natal and attended the University of Natal in the early 1960s. He began his career as a teacher and administrator in South Africa in 1965 and has held various positions in Zambia, Ghana, and the UK, including chief examiner of the West African Examinations Board and academic director of the Teachers Education College in Zambia. After the brutal repression of the Soweto student uprising in 1976, Mr. Samuel returned to South Africa, where he worked as a legal assistant specializing in civil and human rights.

In 1980, Mr. Samuel was appointed the national director of the South African Committee for Higher Education (Sached) Trust, which was formed in 1959 as an innovative response to the crisis in university education created by passage of *The Extension of University Education Act* by the National Party, which closed entry to white universities and established separate universities for African ethnic groups in the 'independent' homelands or Bantustans. An NGO aligned with the ANC, Sached served as the primary center for alternative (non-Bantu) higher education, adult education and training, materials development, distance education, and antiapartheid education.

Mr. Samuel served as the national director of Sached for a decade, until 1990, when he was appointed head of the ANC Education Desk, which was instrumental in developing a national education and training policy. In 1994, following the first democratic elections, in which the ANC became the majority party in the national government, Mr. Samuel was appointed deputy director general of the National Education Department. As deputy director, Mr. Samuel was responsible for developing education policy and legislation, constructing the budget, providing leadership for organizational transformation, restructuring the department, and creating a new Division of Higher Education within the National Department of Education.

In 1998 Mr. Samuel left government to become the senior program director of the W.W. Kellog Foundation, where he worked on an integrated rural

128 *John Samuel*

development program in the eastern highlands of Zimbabwe. Following this, he served in a variety of positions: as an independent education and training consultant and research fellow at the Institute for Interdisciplinary Studies at the University of Stellenbosch and as the chief executive officer of the Nelson Mandela Foundation, the Mandela Rhodes Foundation, and the Oprah Winfrey Leadership Academy for Girls. In 2005 he was selected by the minister of education to head up the National Literacy Initiative. From June 2010 until his retirement in December 2012, Mr. Samuel was the interim director of the Institute for Reconciliation and Social Justice and served as a visiting professor and senior advisor to Jonathan Jansen, the vice chancellor and rector of the UFS.

Mr. Samuel is a cofounder of the South African Campaign – Public Participation in Education Network (PPEN), a citizen's group that works for quality education for all South Africans. He served in senior leadership positions in NGOs, the ANC, the national education department, universities, and private foundations for decades. His extensive and varied experience enables Mr. Samuel to take the long view, to examine contemporary issues in education in South Africa from a historical perspective and from a range of vantage points.

Mr. Samuel coedited a book, *Education: From Poverty to Liberty* (Nasson & Samuel, 1990), which examined the state of education and strategies for reform in South Africa, and has written or coauthored numerous policy reports for international organizations and development agencies such as the United Nations Educational, Scientific and Cultural Organisation (UNESCO).

Mr. Samuel argues that universities occupy a unique public space and thus have a responsibility to be "havens of democratic habits for students" to cultivate a democratic culture and encourage democratic dispositions. As interim director, Mr. Samuel insisted that "the institute locate its work in that critical public space that universities occupy in democratic societies," and identified several strategic aims to drive the work of the institute, which include "helping the university develop the skills, capacities, and practices that will strengthen its ability to respond to the challenges of institutional transformation" (So Long John, p. 12).

Because education policy under apartheid reflected the economic need to control and reproduce an uneducated and unskilled labor force, most blacks were systematically denied access to a basic education. Approximately two thirds of blacks in South Africa received less than six years of schooling, and could therefore be considered illiterate (Samuel, 1991). Thus, Mr. Samuel argued that "the most important educational issue in the evolution of post-apartheid South Africa is the problem of illiteracy and innumeracy" (p. 2). Unless they are an integral part of the reconstruction process, he warned, "[T]he institutions necessary for the creation of a viable and resilient democracy will be stillborn. There cannot be a democracy in a system where the institutions of popular participation are not empowered" (p. 4). Mr. Samuel concluded that "any political or constitutional dispensation in the post-apartheid era that does not systematically dismantle and reconstruct the educational disabilities of the

A new hope   129

majority of South Africans will remain unjust and unequal" (pp. 2, 4). These were prophetic words.

In his view, the long history of racial oppression and exclusion, and inadequate schooling for blacks, must be addressed in the postapartheid era by institutions of higher education, which could serve as incubators for the cultivation of democratic habits and dispositions. The nascent democratic culture that emerged after apartheid must be continually deepened and extended in institutions of higher education by giving students meaningful opportunities to participate in the governance of the university. Mr. Samuel argues that democracy should not be reduced to an abstract ideal relegated to academic discussions but must be an integral practice of public life throughout the university.

For Mr. Samuel, both students and educational leaders have a moral obligation to contribute to making a better, more decent, and more humane society. In contemporary South Africa, the purpose of higher education is not only to prepare students for an occupation but to equip them to participate in creating a better and more just society by cultivating democratic values, habits, and dispositions. Twenty-five years ago Mr. Samuel called on South Africans to "participate in the making of a new destiny" (1991, p. 9). While some progress has been made, there is still much "unfinished business" in fulfilling the promises of the liberation struggle.

Mr. Samuel (hereafter **JS**) began our conversation by talking about how some blacks (a term of racial solidarity that signifies Africans, coloreds, and Indians) during the apartheid era were able to take college courses in an extension program offered by Indiana University (United States) through an arrangement with the South African Committee for Higher Education (Sached) Trust.

JS: We had this project in mind, but we couldn't offer university-level courses because you had to be a university in South Africa. Indiana University ran a really very good extension program in those days; they probably still do. In the course of the discussion this emerged, and at the end of it we had agreed that Indiana University would offer us those extension courses, and we in South Africa would offer an Indiana University-registered recognized course that South African students could do. But the curriculum was designed by us. In that way we got the project off and running. We trained about 1,000 students through that over the 10-year period, many of whom today, including the man who is the mayor of Bloemfontein [the capital of the Free State province], went through that program. It was one of these strange events where just a fortuitous meeting results in something like this happening.

JA: What I'd like to do first is get a sense of your thinking about leadership for social justice, how you understand it, how you think about it, and what it means to you. So, my first question is what does leadership for social justice mean to you? How do you think about it?

JS: Well, I think sometimes we tend to separate these two notions, in fact, and then treat them as two separate things. I think partly this has to do with the

130 *John Samuel*

manner in which over the last 15 or 20 years, notions of leadership training have developed, so the emphasis is, in fact, much more on a set of tricks rather than on substantial issues about what really confronts leaders and leadership, particularly in terms of moral courage. More often than not we separate these two notions, but I think, certainly in my experience, which to a large extent was shaped by my experience of living in this country and the choices that one had to make, began developing an awareness that made me much more conscious of the link between leadership and social justice.

I think it's an issue that one's got to constantly have an interplay between, both at the public level and at the private level. Because, I think, where we are today in the history of this country, we are faced with this huge question about what do we do. We know that the country is drifting away from its mission; we know that. Part of the reason many of us became involved in the antiapartheid struggle was because we believed in a fairer, more decent, more humane society, and therefore our constitution speaks to this. Much of what is embedded in the culture of this country speaks to it, and our own history speaks to it.

So we sit in this rather awkward historical situation, knowing that grand change is not going to happen, so what do we do in the meantime? What kind of moral choices do we make, both at the personal and the public level? Therefore, how do we behave now in ways that don't compromise those values and that mission? That's, in fact, I think, one of the major dilemmas for leadership and social justice at the moment in this country, that we are kind of almost caught in a paralysis.

There is, now with the absence of Mr. Mandela [Nelson Mandela] and Mr. Tutu [Archbishop Desmond Tutu] getting older, and you look for moral courage, and the moral voices in this country, and it's extremely difficult to find it. I think this is partly to do with this almost paralysis, in fact, that we're in, in trying to figure out what is it that we do. What can we do at this stage, both at the personal level, how we live our life from day to day, and the larger moral choices we make with regard to the long-term change in this country?

I see this constant interaction, and certainly in my own life that has been characteristic. I've spent a long time in executive positions in organizations, and almost on a daily basis this notion gets challenged. Because if you don't remind yourself of this, it's quite easy then to get caught in the tricks of running an organization, in getting all the nice details correct but forgetting, in fact, the larger purpose – whether you're running a university, or a school, or a business. It's something that, I think, certainly from my experience, I didn't learn from textbooks. I learned this almost on a daily basis, in fact, through practice, and bringing that practice to bear on my larger understanding of what's happening in society: how it works, what are the currents, what are the undercurrents, and so on.

There's a constant need to make meaning of what is happening to society. This is where, I think, certainly from my experience of interacting with different levels of leadership in this country in different institutions, there's a

A new hope 131

remarkable failure. That this ability to engage with society is almost put on the side, it's almost seen as an irrelevant factor. Only when you're doing a scam, then you bring it in; you do it, and then you forget about it, and then you concentrate on the business of running the organization.

JA: What personal and professional experiences informed your understanding of leadership for social justice? Were there particular moments or experiences that stand out for you? It may or may not happen this way for everyone, but sometimes there are important people or turning points, or particular experiences, that have a large impact on someone's understanding and development. Were there moments like that in your life that were more significant?

JS: I think it's a kind of gradual evolution. I don't think there are any remarkable turning points, as such. My kind of awareness, which relates to the manner in which my notion of social justice developed, started when I was a young boy, living in a little rural town. My parents were fairly religious people; they went to church [the Anglican Church] every Sunday and so on. I'd been to church a number of times, bit it hadn't occurred to me that we were going to two separate services, that when we got to church the white community had left and then there was a service for blacks. I think I must have been around nine or 10 when I kind of figured this out, and I asked my father about this, and he said, "Well that's how things are." and so on – so from that, in fact, that experience.

The second set of shaping experiences, for me, was when I went to university, and again it was racially segregated, even though the university [the University of Natal] itself, the proper university, which had all these noble philosophies and statements and so on. But it actually offered black students physically segregated facilities. This sharp experience of apartheid, in its rawest form, in a context where you had these grand notions of universities – there you are. I'm going to go to university and so on, then, bang, you get hit by this. So starting from a fairly simple moral Christian sort of basis, it sharpened much more into a deeper political and therefore began the search for how do we deal with this. Moralizing about it wasn't going to be enough; having God on your side wasn't going to be enough.

My sense of social justice emerged in that period, in fact, which was lodged with the notion of a better world. To reduce it to its simplicity, a strong notion of fairness, and decency, and a better humanity; it emerged out of that experience. It wasn't something that I sat down and distilled and then said, "Oh yes, I've got a nice view," you know. For the rest of my life, really, until 1994, it was in search of that vision. Whatever I did, wherever I worked, on a daily basis, intellectually, in trying to create organizations, in trying to shape the kind of intellectual climate in the country through different works that we did, and so on, it was informed by this driving ambition to contribute to the creation of a decent society. That's how my notion of social justice was shaped.

Then, of course, in the course of it, you meet individuals and people. Like I was very lucky in the 80s when Archbishop Desmond Tutu chaired Sached.

132 *John Samuel*

Here was somebody who not only occupied a preeminent position in South Africa's struggle but also somebody who was willing to listen to you and discuss things, and so on. That was a very powerful influence because, as chair of Sached, I interacted with him on a large number of issues.

The big dilemma that we tried to manage in Sached was twofold in the sense that there were the immediate victims of apartheid: young children who didn't get an education; teenagers who were excluded from school; adults who had no education, or had very little education, or had disadvantaged opportunities; that kind of thing. You couldn't go to them and say, "Hang on. Wait. The revolution is coming in 20 years' time, and then everything will be sorted out." How do you provide that relief from oppression in ways that go above just simply charity?

Then secondly, in the germ of those ideas, how do you begin thinking about the future? That was the constant kind of dynamic at play in Sached. Our work went from the level of say, for example, we ran what was in those days called a correspondence college, distance education, where young people, young adults who couldn't go to school for a range of different reasons, could get some form of education. We ran probably one of the most successful media projects this country has ever experienced, even now. We published in the Sunday paper; every week for 32 weeks, we published a 24-page educational supplement – 24 pages every week!

JA: I thought that was brilliant.

JS: Students from all over the country, from rural, urban, teachers, students, all participated in it. Khanya College [established in 1986 in Johannesburg to provide education relevant to the needs of historically oppressed communities], for example, was the forward-looking project. This is what a university curriculum would look like in a new South Africa. We had the opportunity to try it out before we came into the new South Africa. All of this, in fact, was shaped by a strong sense of social justice, of the building, of the creation of a better society.

As I said, it went through, certainly my life's experience, as a consistent thread. Even when we set up the institute [the Institute for Reconciliation and Social Justice] here, that was a major informing issue. Then, I think, with the institute now putting social justice in the title, much more strongly than when we started. I think that becomes important because, in a way, *that* remains, for me, one of the unfinished businesses of universities in this country.

Sheer demographics have resulted in larger numbers of blacks coming to universities, so there's been this major shift. But I don't think universities have confronted the social justice issue in the sense that, as in fact, we face this, even within our basic education system. We have done very well in terms of access to education; the vast majority of school-going age children are in school and so on. But I suspect what's happening is that we are cultivating or laying the foundations for a two-class education system in this country.

A new hope 133

There's a smaller section who get a fairly decent education, who do fairly well and whose life chances are improved. But I suspect that there's a larger section of our community that get a third-rate education and who then become part of this vicious cycle.

JA: You mentioned in one of your writings that through the Model C school system, the educational assets of the country have been handed over arbitrarily to a small minority and that they would have to be transferred back into the national pool for a more equitable allocation of resources. You wrote that in 1994. Is that still the case?

JS: I think so. In the main, the objective wasn't to imitate the Model Cs [formerly all-white public schools that are typically well resourced and located mostly in suburban communities]. In other words, we weren't going to take that model and make it applicable to everybody; it was to create a more recruitable model. But I don't think we've achieved that, in fact. Because when we look at the big picture, our educational system, in terms of the conventional measurements like examination results and so on, has been gradually improving. There's no doubt about some of that. But when you begin to break that down and analyze it, in fact, as who are the beneficiaries of the system, I think you get a very different picture.

But the situation at the universities, I think, are somewhat different in that the argument that I've been making, made even here at this university, is that we admit a significantly large number of black students: We're not as good at making them successful. Therefor the social justice issue becomes very important. It's not good enough just simply saying we have an 84% pass rate [the percentage of undergraduate students in public universities who fail their studies and drop out] because, when you look much more closely at it, you'll find, in fact, this university is no different from many other universities.

We have a very high casualty rate at the undergraduate level. I've said this before: If the South African public were only aware of just how badly performing our universities are at the undergraduate level, there will be a huge outcry. The public have this notion that universities are untouchable, so there's this distance between the universities and the general public. When you think of it in terms of issues of equity and social justice, in fact, it's not like we can't afford it. We are spending a significantly large amount of our national resources on higher education, but our spending continues to entrench patterns of past inequalities. But I have not seen a sufficiently encouraging movement by universities, generally, in this country, to address this issue.

JA: In terms of addressing issues of social justice on the campus, what are the major obstacles, forms of resistance, and challenges that social justice leaders face?

JS: I think there's a deadening weight of history and tradition. Universities have remained almost intact from the times of Bologna [the University of Bologna, founded in Bologna, Italy in 1088, is the oldest university in the world],

134 *John Samuel*

and I'm always very cautious about this. I don't believe that we just simply must change things for the sake of changing them. There are certain characteristics of universities that are very important.

I use the word 'conservative,' in that sense, not in the narrow use of the word but the actual act of conserving, of keeping, and practicing, and maintaining. It's independence, the ability to stand above the marketplace and to survive that, in fact, is very important. Its courage derives, I think, in part from that. I mentioned my university, and one of the issues we as undergraduates at the university would often push the authorities on because the authorities would say, "Well, by law, we can't do this." We would say to them, "Well, there's an issue larger than law. Where is the university's moral courage? Why doesn't it take the law on?"

The ability to engage with this notion of: What does it mean? What does the idea of academic freedom mean, not just simply a defense against what I can teach? It's a much larger societal issue in mind. It's a notion that, I think, has been lost, quite honestly in this country; we don't engage with it in that way. I've argued in the past that where we are as a country, at a particular historical moment, and that when we look at the various institutions of democracy, universities are a significant part of those institutions. We have the normal parliament, the press, justice, the courts, etc. Normally we don't think of universities in that context. I argue, in fact, that we must and that when a country is struggling to build its democratic culture, an institution, like a university, is called upon in a historical moment to contribute towards that.

It doesn't happen everywhere; it doesn't happen to every university. There's a unique historical moment in this country that argues for a different role for the university. My sense is that universities haven't stepped up to that challenge. The University of Natal has been styled by people who went to Oxford and Cambridge, so it's this perpetuation of an idea of what a university should be.

JA: The ivory tower verses the engaged university.

JS: Yeah. One gets the sense that it's a debate that happens, to some degree, in the United States, to a lesser degree in Europe and England, to some extent in Australia, I think, and those parts, and to a very lesser extent here in this country. But yet the conditions are probably more appropriate, both in terms of the time and the challenge, to South Africa. We have, for example, two new universities being created [Sol Plaatje University in the Northern Cape and the University of Mpumalanga]. A couple of years ago I said to the minister [of education], "You have a unique opportunity for shaping a South African university. But what are we doing? We're ending up with a hodge-podge, a third-rate imitation of Wits [the University of Witwatersrand] and Cape Town [the University of Cape Town]."

This is where it comes back to the theme of social justice. It's not social justice in some airy-fairy notion on the issues of equity, of resources, of curriculum, of teaching, research. All of these become an integral part that has to be located in the framework of how do we help build a more decent South African society. Our constitution enjoins us to do that. It's a consistent theme; it's not an accident. I was around then; it's not an accident. The constitution is not a document that just emerged out of nowhere. Its singular lesson is that we've lived a particular experience of oppression in this country. How do we avoid recreating that?

The only way to do that is, in fact, to begin talking about a new kind of humanity, if anybody has the chance. I'm not saying we've lost it entirely; if anybody has the chance, it's South Africa. I think it's the weight of tradition and conservatism and just the moral courage to say we need to think differently here. The leadership at higher education is absent; you have one or two people. You have Jonathan [Jansen] here; it's a voice alone. You need more people at different levels, in fact, in the intellectual world of this country.

JA: You talked about your experience going to church as a young person. Do religious beliefs inform your understanding of leadership for social justice? You said that's where your awakening happened; initially it was through Christian values. Do those values continue to have an important influence on your thinking?

JS: No. When I look back, in fact, with a bit of hindsight, I constantly engaged in the act of making sense of things. Why were things like this? For a while, growing up, from about 12 to 16, before I went to university, Christianity and its moral code was a handy reference. It enabled me to divide the world neatly between the good and the bad. In this case, it was the Afrikaners and apartheid that were bad. Then on the other side was the religious: If you prayed hard enough and so on, things will come right. It was a framework that enabled me to make sense, to give meaning to my life on a daily basis.

But by the time I got to university, I was beginning to wonder about this. Then, of course, in 1960 at university, after Sharpeville [the African township where police killed 69 unarmed people demonstrating against pass laws], major urban areas of South Africa erupted – huge marches and so on – and I was witness to the killing of some demonstrators. That act, more than anything else, in fact, told me that it was not good enough just simply to be able to morally condemn. That then changed, made certain kinds of choices important.

At that stage, in my second year of university, my parents and members of the Anglican Church were looking for young, bright blacks; they didn't have too many in the Church. The bishop, there were two of us, offered us scholarships to go read theology at Cambridge. My friend accepted it, and I turned it down because that was a point in my life where I was beginning to become a lot more aware of the complexity of living in this country and the need to, in a way, go beyond just simply finding answers in religion. That's why I turned it down; it was just hypocrisy. I could have gone on to Cambridge, but I chose not to.

JA: Did the emergence of the Black Consciousness Movement affect your thinking in a significant way?

136 John Samuel

JS: Yes, but at that stage, in fact, I'd already left South Africa and was living in Zambia then. It's fascinating, in fact; my kind of route to the Black Consciousness in South Africa was via the Black Consciousness Movement in America. Before I became aware of what was going on in this country, because I was living in Zambia, I was reading a lot of American stuff that was in a way tied to what I had started with when I was in South Africa. Living in South Africa, even as a black, you thought of Africa as this dark continent. You knew nothing about its history; you knew nothing about its ancient culture and traditions, the role of Africa in the world, and so on. When I got to Zambia, all of sudden it opened up to me, so that was another thread that was absent in my education in South Africa. But my awareness about Black Consciousness was prompted to a large extent, initially, by the Americans we read.

It influenced me without my knowing it was already doing the same thing in South Africa. Then, of course, as stuff began emerging, I would be in touch with people and so on. It was probably the most significant factor that influenced my decision to come back to South Africa. I saw a turning point that hadn't been there before, this sense that we could overcome was already beginning. Then, of course, 1976 happened [the Soweto student uprising, which was brutally repressed by the police]. I was at a college in Zambia; I was training teachers. I then said, "That's it." In 1977 I came back to South Africa and got involved with the Black Consciousness Movement.

The interesting thing was that I'd taken up my legal studies, was working as a professional assistant with the firm that was the instructing attorneys for the Biko family [Steve Biko, who played a leading role in the formation and intellectual development of the Black Consciousness Movement, was killed by the police in 1977]. We, in fact, then handled the inquest because his wife instructed us, as the attorneys, to represent them at the inquest. But it was, in fact, this realization that the emergence of a movement like Black Consciousness was deeper than just simply political. It represented a significant shift in the mental paradigm of the oppressed in this country; there was no turning back. That was, for me, the turning point.

JA: People talk about that period as a sort of politically calm period. Not too much was going on, but yet this ferment, this consciousness, was laying the groundwork for what came afterwards.

JS: Yes, at one level it might have been quiet, but the undercurrents were pretty intense.

JA: I came across something that you wrote when Neville Alexander retired. In your tribute to Neville, who was apparently a very close friend of yours [he passed away in 2012], you say, "In the words of [Bertolt] Brecht, Neville is someone who brings passion and reason; the short-term perspective and the long-term view; cold patience and infinite perseverance; anger and tenacity in the struggle to build a better world" (Samuel, n.d.). I was struck by your description. Can you elaborate on how this view informs your thinking about leadership and change?

JS: In a way what I'm trying to get at, in fact, it's a set of different experiences, of lived experiences, that helps you begin to make meaning of life and society. There is, then, direct interaction with leadership if you're in that position, and there is a constant interaction between these two things. What I've found, in fact, is that we often are reluctant to draw on that. We don't, in a way, mine that richness; say how do I use this in my running of this university, in my running of this organization? At Sached, for example, when I took over in 1980 as the national director, I didn't know a thing about running an organization. I hadn't been to business school; I hadn't read any textbooks and so on. Almost on a daily basis we were shaping an organization where mission and purpose were just as important as the strategic plan and the budget.

For example, one of the things that I did as the chief executive, I held weekly meetings with all my senior staff: So priority number one was this. I kind of came across this accidentally. Nobody told me this, but I knew that what was important in an organization at that time was this engagement, the intellectual challenging, the solidarity, the comradeship. These were important. Instinctively I knew that, though I was trying to give it form, organizational form and shape, and it took that form, these weekly meetings. On both sides there was an understanding that you didn't miss this. I don't care what you were doing; this was very important. We then shaped a convention, which happened twice a year, which was like almost reps from different sections of the organization from different parts of the country. We met in one central venue, and the organization was discussed and that sort of thing.

Today that may look pretty obvious, but in the 80s it wasn't. All of this was being shaped by the notion that, well, here we are trying to argue for a better world and so on. How do you make a better organization? That was a constant, I think, partly because Sached was an NGO; we weren't paying princely salaries. A lot of people, professional people like Neville Alexander – there was Enver Motala. Neville could have walked into a university. Many of my other colleagues had professions: lawyers, academics. Adam Habib, who's now at Wits University [he is the Vice chancellor of the University of Witwatersrand], he worked at Sached. I mean, when you look at the Sached staffing list today. I will never forget it, in fact, the first meeting of the heads of education departments in the independent government in 1994; of 10 people in the room, eight were Sached staff.

JA: Sached was really an incubator for leadership that then sort of blossomed.

JS: Yea, very much so, in fact. I've always maintained that our programs might have been very good, but our people were one of the proudest things that we achieved. Coming back to this, it's in a way related to Melanie Walker's work [the director of the Center for Research on Higher Education & Development at the UFS] where she's trying to go beyond the skills level, ask other questions – Sen's [Amartya Sen] notion of capabilities. I suspect there's quite a useful opening there. I've always said to people, you can teach a monkey to perform a set of tricks, but it still won't make the monkey a leader.

138 *John Samuel*

The other notion I constantly struggle with is that we can't just simply rely on, for example, the way in which I learned my leadership skills; it was trial and error. How do we begin pulling it out? How do we begin pulling the lessons and so on out? You know I don't have any answers for that. I come back to this notion that you must begin to lodge yourself in some real experiences that help shape you as a leader. Balancing that, in fact, is very important, like when I worked with Mr. Mandela to help set up the Mandela Foundation. Had I been younger, I probably would have managed it differently because I have the advantage of age and experience with me. You know, when you work for a global icon like Mr. Mandela, one of the temptations, because the power is so great, is for you to be seduced by the power eventually. I've seen this; I've interacted with people like that, who work for very powerful people. Although these people are powerful, they themselves are not necessarily full of egos and so on, but the people around them acquire a certain kind of pound of greatness. You know, I've seen it so many times.

When I worked for Mr. Mandela I was very conscious of this, and very conscious of it personally, but also in terms of my staff. I would constantly remind them that it's not about you; it's about Mr. Mandela. Our job is to make him look good. Leadership is very often challenged in that way, and if there's no grounding, you can begin to believe that you're great. I've seen this, again, happen to so many people. Then the gap between you and the reality grows. Our former president is a very good example of that; Thabo Mbeki, where he lost touch with that reality, didn't even know that people were organizing against him.

JA: Ben Turok talks about that in his book (Turok, 2014). They [Mbeki and his supporters] thought they were going to win. Even after this huge outpouring of pro-Zuma support [Jacob Zuma was elected head of the ANC in 2007], they still thought they were going to win.

JS: Right. You know Greenleaf (Greenleaf, 1977), who writes about servant leadership? It's a very powerful notion of leadership, in fact, that if you don't understand following, you will not become a leader, or you'll become a bad leader. That, quite often, I think, is one of the drawbacks to leadership. We forget that part of it, and we emphasize the greatness notion. When I was in government, the idea that you could formulate a policy that affects the lives of millions of people – I had in my office a picture of a classroom with kids to constantly remind myself and the people who work with me: That's who we should have in mind when we formulate policy; *that's* who we should have in mind, so that we keep touch.

You know, going into government in 1994, I'd worked in the Ministry [of Education] when I worked in Zambia, so I had some notions of government and so on. But for the vast majority of us going into government in 1994, we hadn't a clue. Suddenly, you have this enormous power; you didn't think carefully about it. It could be grading pieces of legislation that are going to be effective for the next 20 years; that is very powerful and very seductive. I know in some instances it paralyzed some of our people because they were so frightened of doing anything, and as a result of that, nothing actually happened; you have that side of it as well.

JA: You hear a lot of talk these days about transformation. People use that term. It gets bandied about and has lots of different meanings for different people. I know it's been politicized. But what does that mean for you? What does transformation at this institution mean for you, and what would that look like?

JS: I must say, I've become a transformation cynic partly because of the way we use the word, shifted its meaning, used its currency, and the PR [public relations] of the label transformation. Part of it, I suspect, has got to do with our reluctance to have the real kind of intellectual engagement, honest and open, that at one time characterized the intellectual life of this country but is absent today. This is part of the reason why charlatans get away with transformation means X. Nothing, I think, is more debasing than to give a standard definition.

In a way, I think, partly because of that, which is regrettable, the minister [of higher education] has decided to set up a transformation committee. I can understand part of the reason for that. I suspect part of the reason was that he was hoping this would come from the universities, but it didn't, or at least it didn't appear to come from the universities. Interestingly, in fact, in the period when Thabo Mbeki was president, he was also deeply concerned about what was going on at our universities at a deeper level – the meaning of universities in South Africa and so on. He asked the minister – it wasn't then higher education; that was created later [the Ministry of Higher Education and Training was created in 2010] – in fact, and nothing came of it. The minister, then, was supposed to contact all the leading universities and ask them to write a paper for the president: What should the role of a new South African university be? Thabo Mbeki eventually got back to us and said, "It looks like you all can't do this; I'm going to do it myself." He did; he produced a 20 pager. It didn't go very far because bureaucrats at universities, officials, and heads, and so on, can stall things if they want to, so it just died and then the presidency.

There's an absence of a real intellectual engagement with this issue that needs to go deeper. I mean there are important external factors: opposition, academic staffing, etc. But all of that's got to be informed by some deeper purpose: Why do we want more academics in the humanities and that kind of thing? What is higher education's notion of South African society? What do we mean by a more humane society?

The constitution urges us towards a particular vision. How do we give substance to that vision? How do I teach, for example, law, that will enable me now as a lawyer to practice law in a way that doesn't build only on the notion that if you break a contract, or who are the parties to the contract. Where does fairness come into play? Where do these other notions of social justice?

140 *John Samuel*

I've spent a while at this university. The irony is that, and I don't think the UFS is the exception, a student taking a law degree at this university can go through four years without encountering the notion of social justice.

JA: They have no courses that address issues of social justice?

JS: They do have some, but it's quite often an elective, an option. But that's one of the misfits at the moment in the country: The legal system lags behind the social-political system of the country. That's transformation for me: How do we transform the law degree, where the emphasis, in fact, on the current law degree is on private and personal law, not on social law. How do we strike a balance? Obviously, you have to have that. There are individuals in society, and the law has got to protect us in that way, but also there is wider social law. How do we begin bringing that into the curriculum? Where do we strike the balance between fairness and contract? These are big, important questions that, in a way, our Constitutional Court has already set the example. Where before you could just simply evict somebody from a house, the Constitutional Court said you can't do that now; that person has the right to live. Therefore, if you want to evict them, they have to have an alternative place to live.

But there's that lag between our curriculum and the part that the Constitutional Court is pointing. That, for me, would be transformation: the new law curriculum. Or at another level, take the way the university does business, the role of students within that. We have SRCs [Student Representative Councils are elected bodies that represent the interests of students], but there is no real engagement of students in terms of issues of running a university. That, again, would be an example of transformation; students are involved in a more substantial way in the governance of the university. Universities are run primarily as private entities. They're extremely powerful in that sense, and that's one of the reasons why the public knows very little.

Now you take this whole issue of social justice, equity. A large number of our students, particularly black students, struggle to keep themselves together financially, for example, having to make the choice: Do I pay for bus fare to travel to university, or do I have a meal? I know because I've worked in the inside of the beast, both in government and outside of government: Universities spend, quite often unnecessarily, on a range of things.

I'll just give you this example. When I was setting up the institute I caused quite a bother because I refused to accept a new consignment of furniture that was in keeping with the university's standards. I said, "Well, if somebody can come and explain to me and justify all of this, I'll accept it." Of course, they couldn't because somebody must have been getting a side cut somewhere from some furniture supplier and so on. In the end, in fact, what I did was I went into the provisioning department and got solid wooden desks, which were perfectly functional, and they still are at the institute, that furniture. I'm not saying that these are significant things in and of themselves, but when added to a whole lot of other things, they do have meaning because this is public money we are spending.

A new hope 141

I know it from the inside: I ran higher education in this country. I was intimately involved in the financing of the universities. I knew that if I took a 10% cut of the budget of the university, they'll survive; I knew that. But, again, what it means is: Are universities asking themselves some of those deeper financial questions? If we're pursuing equity, how is it reflected in the way we allocate our resources? I'm not just saying go and buy wooden furniture just for the sake of it. But these would then become real issues; these questions would be located in a particular context of asking about how we're spending our money.

It then relates to, in fact, where we can then say we can support 300 or 400 students through a food subsidy; that would be transformation. The other issue which I've been in constant discussions over here with students is the possibility of starting a student co-op, which is run by students, where they cut the middleman out and they service the student body, because the internal economy of the university is pretty high. When you look at the money students spend on our campus, you're talking about millions. Why should that benefit a third party? There are successful examples of student co-ops throughout the world, including housing courts. That would be an example of transformation.

JA: You've been doing this work for a very long time. It's clear that you have a moral purpose, but you must have hit lots of bumps along the way and sometimes probably got knocked pretty hard. What keeps you going in the face of the different kinds of resistance to change that you've been talking about, to create the conditions for social justice?

JS: It's the same question that people used to ask us in the antiapartheid days. There was no way we're going to shift this government with the military capacity it had, the security apparatus, etc. I suppose, you know, there is this lingering notion that we can do better: This just can't be what we should be happy with. There's that lingering notion, in fact. Therefore, first of all, you take the long-term view. But secondly, it's informed by understanding that nothing, even the mighty Soviet Union, lasts forever. If you can't take hope from that, you may as well give up. No system that has been created can last forever. It is in the nature of human civilization that things change; that's the way we progress, constantly in search of something better. It's a very difficult idea to hold onto because there are so many different ways you can be made to detour from that idea. We need more and more people to begin to believe in this, not to give up on that, because that's the way we sustain it; that's the way we keep it going.

Significance and implications

Mr. Samuel's leadership has always been driven by a vision of a more decent and humane society, a moral vision grounded in an abiding desire for social justice and to serve the public good. He is a servant leader who leads by following and

142 *John Samuel*

cultivating the capabilities of others, an "old warrior" who "rages on" to complete the "unfinished business" of the liberation struggle (Samuel, n.d.). Mr. Samuel argues that institutions of higher education in contemporary South Africa play crucial roles as incubators of democracy in fostering the habits of mind and dispositions that make a democratic culture possible.

In his view, transformation is concerned with cultivating an ethos of social justice as a guiding principle of educational policy, practice, and leadership, and with meeting the needs of the least privileged in society. Mr. Samuel argues that institutions of higher education in South Africa need more voices of moral courage, leaders who are willing to go against the grain, to stand up for the values and ideals enshrined in the South African Constitution. For him, the crisis of higher education, and of the country, is a largely a crisis of moral leadership, of people who believe in and are committed to creating a more just, decent, and humane society.

References

Greenleaf, R. (1977). *Servant leadership: A journey into the nature of legitimate power and greatness.* New York: Paulist Press.

Nasson, B., & Samuel, J. (Eds.). (1990). *Education: From poverty to liberty.* Cape Town: David Philip.

Samuel, J. (1991). Central challenges in educational reconstruction in post-apartheid South Africa. *International conference on the educational needs of the victims of apartheid in South Africa.* Background paper no. 6. Paris: UNESCO.

Samuel, J. (n.d.). *South African voices, past and present: A tribute to Neville Alexander.* Retrieved from http://www.praesa.org.za/files/2012/07/South-African-Voices-Past-Present2.pdf

So long John and thanks for all the fish. (November, 2012). *Botho: The newsletter of the institute for reconciliation and social justice.* Bloemfontein: University of the Free State.

Turok, B. (2014). *With my head above the parapet: An insider account of the ANC in power.* Auckland Park, SA: Jacana Media.

9 A bigger dream
Visions of educational leadership for transformation and social justice in South Africa

John Ambrosio

What insights and lessons can be gleaned from these narratives about educational leadership for transformation and social justice in contemporary South Africa? What ideas, concepts, values, principles, and ways of thinking can potentially inform the work of other educational leaders in South Africa and elsewhere? As discussed earlier, the concepts of transformation and social justice in educational leadership signify different things to different people in different contexts (Beachum, 2008; Blackmore, 2011; Bogotch, 2002 & 2008; Jansen, 2008; Larson & Murtadha, 2002; Shields, 2010). The meanings ascribed to them are shaped and delimited by the conditions and circumstances in which educational leaders find themselves, by the issues and problems that emerge with a particular context and historical moment. Despite sharing a common institutional context, the various conceptions of leadership for transformation and social justice articulated by these leaders are deeply informed by their diverse lived experiences.

While their perspectives may differ, these educational leaders have one thing in common: a vision of larger purposes, a bigger mission, what Dr. Molebatsi Nkoane calls 'a bigger dream' that undergirds, drives, and sustains their work. They dream of possible worlds in which socially constructed differences, such as race, no longer have significance, in which every person has an opportunity to develop his or her capabilities and lead a healthy and dignified life, in which care, empathy, and compassion prevail over fear, mistrust, and divisiveness, and moral courage and integrity over corruption and turpitude. Visions of a more decent, humane, and just society infuse their leadership with meaning and purpose and propel them forward in difficult times.

These leaders also share a certain ontological relation to the world. They do not simply adopt or adhere to principles of social justice; they embody and live them. For these educational leaders, social justice is not simply a question of embracing a particular set of values and beliefs but a way of life, a way of being in the world. Their approach to leadership is a manifestation of their identities, core values and beliefs, and ethical commitments, and thus is less a conscious choice, a deliberate or intentional act, than second nature, an organic expression of who they have become and are becoming.

Many of these educational leaders are strongly influenced and motivated by religious values, beliefs, and traditions that provide a kind of foundational ethics

144   John Ambrosio

for their leadership. Whether or not religion plays an important role in informing their thought and practice, these leaders draw on a variety of theoretical approaches, including neo-Marxism, post-structuralism, critical theory, post-colonialism, and psychoanalysis, to understand themselves and others, and the society and world in which they live.

Both Professor Keet and Dr. Lange reimagine educational leadership as a form of citizenship. While academic citizens recognize the diverse identities, aspirations, and ways students engage with the world, and believe they should play a significant role in driving the transformation process, republican citizens seek to cultivate the capacity of students for agency and public deliberation. Both conceptions require educational leaders to reimagine their relation to students, whether by viewing them as subjects of change rather than objects of regulation and management or by providing students with opportunities to practice moral reasoning and decision-making. Educational leaders who are academic citizens also have a responsibility to create a safe, welcoming, and inclusive campus culture, to articulate and represent the core values, purposes, and vision of the university, and to make them a visible and ubiquitous presence in the everyday experience of students, staff, and administrators.

The notion of 'servant leadership' discussed by Mr. Samuel is fundamental to how these educational leaders think about their practice. According to Greenleaf (1977), who coined the term, "the servant as leader" always seeks to prioritize the needs of others, to serve their interests first. In his view, the difference between a servant-first and a leader-first approach "is the care taken by the servant-first to make sure that other people's highest priority needs are being served; that they grow as persons while being served; that they become healthier, wiser, freer, more autonomous, more likely themselves to become servants" (pp. 13–14). In other words, servant-first leaders act out of a genuine desire to serve others and enable them to lead flourishing lives. Servant-first leaders are also deeply concerned with how their actions affect the poor and the least privileged in society, and have "an overarching purpose, a big dream, a visionary concept" that motivates their leadership (pp. 14–15).

Professor Mahlomaholo's notion of 'invitational leadership' is a kind of servant leadership in that it aims to foster the personal growth and professional development of students and faculty by ensuring equity and fairness in the allocation of resources and opportunities, especially for people who were previously marginalized and excluded. He strongly believes that people are more productive when they want to be, rather than when they have to be, that honoring the trust a leader places in them is a greater incentive to increase the quality of their work and scholarly productivity than the fear of failure or punishment. Thus, invitational leadership requires trust and a leap of faith, the belief that students and faculty will respond positively to being treated with respect and will, over time, become increasingly productive. In an international context dominated by the neoliberal discourse of testing and accountability, of labeling and punishment, the notion of invitational leadership takes a different view: The most humane and effective way to motivate faculty and students to produce high-quality work is to provide them with the support and resources that enable them to be successful.

Professor Keet argues that administrators should not seek to impose an abstract value structure on students, that the values they want students to accept and embrace must already be observable in their classes and lectures, in curricula, at public events, and in their relations with the administration. He insists that educational leaders must build on what is already empirically present in the lived experience of students before seeking to introduce unfamiliar values and should listen carefully to students, not only to give them an opportunity to express their views but because their participation in the transformation process is essential to its success. Similarly, Reverend Buys insists that administrators should not impose a hierarchy of values on students, but focus instead on cultivating a community of shared aspirations driven by values, through a deliberative process that does not privilege the values of either party.

A number of these leaders argue that students should be empowered to play a more significant role in university governance, in curriculum design, and in establishing new cultural traditions. Dr. Lange argues that students have the right and the responsibility to critique forms of disciplinary knowledge diffused by the university and demand access to alternative kinds of knowledge; Reverend Buys argues that students should be given opportunities to establish new cultural traditions in residence halls, and Mr. Samuel insists that students should play a greater role in university governance. For them, transforming the institutional culture of the university requires that students play a more meaningful role in shaping their educational experience.

Professor Jansen argues that the capacity for self-doubt and critique is essential to leadership for transformation and social justice, that self-knowledge and understanding, and the ability to accurately assess one's actions and, when necessary, to change course to correct one's mistakes, are key attributes of good leaders. Since making mistakes is an inevitable aspect of leadership, the willingness to acknowledge one's errors, and to rectify them, is crucial. For these reasons, educational leaders need to allow themselves to evolve over time, to change their thinking and practice in accordance with new insights, experiences, and conditions, and develop an openness to the critiques of others, which make it possible to arrive at better decisions.

Transformative leaders accept the certainty that they will make mistakes, that their emotions, unconscious biases, and experiences will weigh heavily on their thinking and decision-making. The question, then, is not whether educational leaders will make mistakes but how they will respond to the inevitability of making them. Leaders who are unable to tolerate self-doubt or uncertainty, or engage in a genuine process of self-critique, will likely repeat their mistakes.

Reverend Buys engaged in such a process when he questioned and reassessed his approach to ending the tradition called *tikkie*, which involved showering female students in the residence halls. The vehement protests of the mostly Afrikaner students and their supporters led Reverend Buys to rethink his actions and recognize his mistake in assuming that the relationship between administrators

146   *John Ambrosio*

and students had fundamentally changed, that it was no longer adversarial or based on asymmetrical relations of power, because students were involved in the transformation process. This insight led Reverend Buys to argue that students and administrators need to move beyond an adversarial relationship in which they compete for power, to one that seeks to foster a community of shared aspirations driven by values, rather than based on them.

As might be expected, the demographic differences among these educational leaders affected their experience of leadership at the UFS. For the older leaders, their conception of transformation and social justice is framed primarily by their experience of apartheid and the liberation struggle, while younger leaders were more deeply influenced by the struggles of the postapartheid era. Reverend Buys, whose lived experience straddled this generational divide, discussed his experience of having to shoulder the double burden of being an Afrikaner and a minister in the Dutch Reformed Church and how this historical baggage prevented him from playing a more significant leadership role in the transformation process. Dr. Lange discussed her experience of often being the only woman at meetings of senior management, of having to continually navigate the patriarchal dispositions of the mostly older Afrikaner men who still dominate higher-level administrative positions at the UFS. And as Professor Mahlomaholo made clear, the question of race remains a major issue for black leaders at the UFS. White supremacy did not disappear after the end of apartheid; it simply moved underground. Thus, while overt acts of white racism are no longer acceptable, subtle, covert, and insidious forms of racism, such as micro-aggressions, are an everyday reality for black leaders.

Many leaders argued that the concept of transformation should not be reduced to numbers, that is, *only* to issues of equity, but should also focus on transforming the kinds of disciplinary knowledge, curricula, pedagogical practices, normative values, and social relations of the university. For them, deep transformation is not simply about redress, about replacing one social group with another, but about thinking differently, about challenging and displacing self-evident truths and taken-for-granted assumptions about the nature and purpose of higher education, about changing its underlying value structure and moral imperatives.

Thus, while it is essential that leadership at all levels of the UFS more accurately reflect the demographic makeup of the country, Professor Jansen argues that the racial assignment or gender identity of a leader is less important in driving the transformation process in a progressive direction, in changing inherited patterns of knowledge and dominant ways of thinking, than her or his core values, beliefs, and ethical commitments.

For Professor Mahlomaholo, transformation has a human and a material dimension: fostering mutual respect in social relations and ensuring the equitable distribution of opportunities and resources. Similarly, Mr. Samuel argues that changing the material conditions of life for students, such as providing those in greatest need with adequate food (the No Student Hungry Program, established by Professor Jansen, provides some students with a daily stipend for food), is transformative. In his view, refusing to spend public funds on unnecessary items like new furniture; changing the law school curriculum to require students to take courses that focus on social justice; and creating co-ops to provide students with access to lower-cost food, books and academic supplies, and housing are transformative because they serve the interests of students, especially the most disadvantaged.

A number of key terms emerged in the narratives, which include the concepts of brokenness, vulnerability, complicity, and forgiveness. These notions are based on the premise that all leaders are fallible, that despite their best efforts and intentions, they will make mistakes because they are broken people who are imperfect and carry the burdens and limitations of their histories, identities, and lived experiences. As Mr. Samuel reminds us, the pressing weight of history and tradition can be a significant obstacle to progressive change, especially in a post-conflict society grappling with historical memory and trauma.

As Professor Keet argued, no one is innocent; everyone is complicit, to some degree, with the forces of privilege and oppression in society, including those who participated in the liberation struggle. History, he insists, is messy and makes it impossible to simply divide the world into perpetrators and victims, despite the fact that the apartheid system was unequivocally evil. Acknowledging one's complicity in the web of privilege and oppression, in perpetuating institutions, narratives, and social practices that benefit some individuals and groups while disadvantaging others, opens up the possibility of seeing other people differently, and of forgiving them, since we ourselves must also be forgiven.

This is precisely what Professor Gobodo-Madikizela did in the case of the Truth and Reconciliation Commission when she insisted that the voices of some white soldiers in the South African Defense Force be included in the hearings and that the suffering of white mothers who lost children in the conflict also be acknowledged. Rather than see the world strictly in terms of white perpetrators and black victims, Professor Gobodo-Madikizela thought it was important to recognize that some white soldiers served reluctantly and did not necessarily share the racial ideology of Afrikaner nationalism and that some blacks strongly supported Bantustan governments and inflicted great harm and suffering on other blacks.

This is *not* to say that the two situations are morally equivalent, or that black violence is unrelated to the long history and legacy of colonialism, apartheid, and the physical, psychic, emotional, and cultural damage it inflicted on black people, but simply that no one can claim innocence to not being complicit, in some way, to some degree, in the historical trauma suffered by black and white South Africans. Taking such a stand requires great moral courage, especially at a time when many blacks, who were brutalized and suffered horrific violence during the apartheid era, called for severe punishment rather than understanding and forgiveness.

Professor Gobodo-Madikizela argues that forgiveness is essential for educational leaders and others in post-conflict societies where people must live with historical memory and trauma and with the perpetrators of violence. As Professor Jansen explained, he can forgive others because he has been forgiven, because his evangelical Christian faith and recognition of his own brokenness enable him to lead. Acknowledging our inherent limitations as human beings can also produce a sense of humility and an openness to the views of other

148 *John Ambrosio*

similarly broken and complicit people. Acknowledging one's brokenness makes it possible to lead because, as Professor Jansen argued, at best we colead: we cannot do it alone.

Of course, these attributes of leadership may seem perplexing when compared to corporate models, which are based on the view that effective leaders must create an image of absolute certainty and be unyielding in their decisions. As Professor Jansen argues, the notion of the great man or woman, of the solitary and decisive leader, is nonsense and actually undermines good leadership. Paradoxically, embracing our vulnerabilities and limitations as human beings can lead to better decisions because it allows a variety of ideas to emerge in deliberations with others who are viewed as coleaders rather than followers.

As these narratives indicate, a crucial quality of leadership is the ability and willingness to demonstrate moral courage in decision-making, to make difficult decisions in situations where the way forward is ambiguous, uncertain, and will likely result in recriminations. These educational leaders always seek to do what is good and what is right, often at their own expense and that of their families, and sometimes as the lone voice in an unsupportive or hostile environment. They take personal and professional risks to protect and promote the values and ethical commitments they cherish and hold dear.

Reverend Buys demonstrated moral courage by allowing himself to evolve, to change his thinking and approach to implementing a cultural change program at a historically Afrikaner residence hall. This quality of leadership was also evident in Dr. Lange's critical self-examination and reappraisal of how she communicated her dissatisfaction with the job performance of a black colleague, in Professor Gobobo-Madikizela's insistence that white soldiers be included in the hearings of the Truth and Reconciliation Commission, and when Professor Jansen took the bold step of not expelling the white students involved in the Reitz incident. In each of these cases, doing what was morally consistent with their core values, beliefs, and principles, took precedence over taking the convenient or uncontroversial course of action.

The purpose of this book is not to enumerate a set of essential practices that administrators can adopt to become transformative leaders, or produce a manual for professional practice, but to give readers a portal into the lives and thoughts of some educational leaders who are committed to transformation and social justice at a leading institution of higher education in South Africa. My aim is to enable readers to gain new insights from these narratives; to provide them with a repertoire of ideas, concepts, and ways of thinking and acting that can inform their leadership and illuminate new pathways toward possible futures.

As Mr. Samuel, Professor Gobodo-Madikizela and others have argued, there is a dearth of morally courageous leaders in institutions of higher education and other sectors of South African society, as there is globally. Unfortunately, many individuals lead short of their deepest convictions because they fear the potential consequences of taking controversial or unpopular positions, of taking risks that might jeopardize their financial security or career aspirations. Thus, one of the great challenges of practicing leadership for transformation and social justice in

A bigger dream 149

contemporary South Africa is to reach beyond one's fears and perceived self-interest and embrace the better versions of ourselves.

We can find inspiration for this in the example of individuals who have led exemplary lives fighting for a more just and decent society. In his inaugural address at the UFS, Professor Jansen pointed to the example of Bram Fischer, an Afrikaner lawyer who represented leaders of the liberation struggle and tirelessly fought against the apartheid regime, as someone whose extraordinary life and legacy could serve as a model for other South Africans. Bram Fischer's life reminds us of the potential we all have to move beyond the limits of normative discourses and constraining notions of group identity to live our most deeply held values and convictions. Perhaps most importantly, embracing the better versions of ourselves enables us to imagine the same possibility in others, as Nelson Mandela did with his prison guards at Robben Island.

As Professor Jansen noted, "The closest analogy to the university of the Free State is actually the University of Mississippi. They have exactly the same issues; having been baptized in the language of slavery, and segregation, and Jim Crow, and so on." The reason for this racial symmetry is that both universities are situated in national contexts marked by a long history of racial oppression. The University of Mississippi is located in a former Confederate state in the Deep South that fiercely resisted racial integration in the early 1960s and terrorized blacks with savage violence. Given that a form of racial apartheid existed in both countries for many years, and both universities are historically white institutions, it is not surprising that they have similar racial dynamics and issues regarding the persistence of white supremacy.

The fact that white racism remains an everyday reality at both universities is evident in the racial incidents at the UFS previously discussed and in the recent (2014) discovery of a noose around the neck of a campus statue of James Meridith, an African American man who integrated the university in 1962, which was found along with a former Georgia state flag with a Confederate battle emblem. The intergenerational transfer of historical memory and trauma in both cases make achieving racial reconciliation and social justice an ongoing challenge for educational leaders. Because institutions of higher education with similar racial histories exist in other countries, the insights and lessons gleaned from these narratives may have implications for educational leaders elsewhere, especially where racialized capitalism has deep roots.

University initiatives like the F1 Leadership for Change study abroad program, which sends a group of first-year students to universities abroad each year to learn about other cultures; the Prestige Scholars' program, which provides some newer faculty with research assistance, financial support, and faculty mentors; and the No Student Hungry Program, which provides some students with a daily stipend for food are examples of transformative programs at the UFS that universities in other highly unequal, post-conflict societies might find useful in addressing their own particular needs and circumstances.

To accelerate the process of transformation and give young scholars an opportunity to begin their academic careers, Professor Jansen instituted a mandatory

150 John Ambrosio

retirement age of 60 for most faculty. While this was not a welcome policy for older faculty, most of whom are white Afrikaner men, it is another example of Professor Jansen having the moral courage to make a difficult decision to move the transformation process forward. As these leaders have repeatedly demonstrated, there are no easy answers to the difficult question of how to advance the process institutional transformation and social justice. There are always trade-offs: something is always gained and something is lost; some individuals and groups benefit, while others do not, in most policy decisions. Nonetheless, these educational leaders continue to make the difficult choices, navigating the turbulent waters of seeking both social cohesion and social justice, reconciliation *and* redress.

References

Beachum, F. (2008). Toward a transformational theory of social justice. In I. Bogotch et al. (Eds.), *Radicalizing educational leadership: Dimensions of social justice* (pp. 39–60). Rotterdam: Sense Publishers.

Blackmore, J. (2011). Leadership in pursuit of purpose: Social, economic, and political transformation. In C. Shields (Ed.), *Transformative leadership: A reader* (pp. 21–36). New York: Peter Lang.

Bogotch, I. (2002). Educational leadership and social justice: Theory into practice. *Journal of School Leadership*, 12(2), 138–156.

Bogotch, I. (2014). Educational theory: The specific case of social justice as an educational leadership construct. In I. Bogotch & C. Shields (Eds.), *International handbook of educational leadership and social (in)justice* (Vol. 1) (pp. 51–66). New York: Springer.

Jansen, J. (2008). The challenge of the ordinary. In I. Bogotch et al. (Eds.), *Radicalizing educational leadership: Dimensions of social justice* (pp. 147–156). Rotterdam: Sense Publishers.

Larson, C. & Murtadha, K. (2002). Leadership for social justice. In J. Murphy (Ed.), *The educational leadership challenge: Redefining leadership for the 21st century* (pp. 134–161). Yearbook of the National Society for the Study of Education. Chicago: University of Chicago Press.

Shields, C. (2010). Transformative leadership: Working for equity in diverse contexts. *Educational Administration Quarterly*, 46(4), 558–589.